Achiev

QTS

meeting the **professional standards framework**

Teaching
Primary Art
and Design

Achieving
QTS

meeting the **professional standards framework**

Teaching
Primary Art
and Design

Paul Key with Jayne Stillman

www.learningmatters.co.uk

Acknowledgements

The authors would like to thank the artists, adults and children who have contributed work, including those from Hampshire schools: The Butts School, Sun Hill Infant School and Trosnant Junior School. Thanks also to the students at the University of Winchester, and to Arthur and Ava, for timely reminders to notice and value young children's ideas and actions.

Progression charts on pages 67–71 reproduced with the kind permission of HIAS, Hampshire County Council.

First published in 2009 by Learning Matters Ltd.

British Library Cataloguing in Publication Data
A CIP record for this book is available from the British Library.

ISBN 978 1 84445 254 5

Cover design by Topics – The Creative Partnership
Text design by Code 5 Design Associates Ltd
Project management by Deer Park Productions, Tavistock
Typeset by PDQ Typesetting Ltd, Newcastle-under-Lyme
Printed and bound in Great Britain by Bell & Bain Ltd, Glasgow

Learning Matters Ltd
33 Southernhay East
Exeter EX1 1NX
Tel: 01392 215560
info@learningmatters.co.uk
www.learningmatters.co.uk

Contents

The authors

Paul Key is Senior Lecturer at the University of Winchester teaching primary art and design education. He has teaching experience in both primary and secondary schools. He is currently the Subject Coordinator for Primary Art and Design Education at the University of Winchester and has ten years' experience in Higher Education. He is a past Chair of NSEAD Teacher Education Board and currently participates in the Higher Education the Arts and Schools (HEARTS) project, a national initiative to promote primary school arts teaching through ITT. His artistic and professional interests led him to complete an MA in printmaking, as part of the Artist-Teacher Scheme.

Jayne Stillman is currently the County Inspector/Adviser for Visual and Performance Arts in Hampshire. She supports primary, secondary and special schools in the LA. She is an associate lecturer at the University of Winchester where she supports teachers with units for MA (Education), alongside this she is a research student. She has previously been a moderator and team leader for GCSE examinations and also a Regional Subject Adviser with the NSEAD for the New Secondary Curriculum.

Introduction

Aims and organisation

This book aims to help you towards teaching purposeful and imaginative art and design in primary schools. It is written in a spirit which embraces the idea that art and design teaching and learning, and art and design practice, share characteristics. They can be described in similar ways, as being:

> *playful, imaginative, personal, cultural, emergent, open, flexible, disciplined, skilful, thoughtful, intelligent, engaging, purposeful, practical, inventive, interesting, expressive.*

The marriage of these varied terms indicates the diverse nature of art and design teaching and learning, and is indicative of the challenges this brings for those who choose to teach. We anticipate that as intending teachers your experiences of, and confidence in, art and design will be varied. The ambition of this book is to recognise your needs, to aspire to the spirit described above, and to maintain that spirit through the following aims:

1. Develop awareness of the possibilities of art and design for young children.
2. Develop awareness of art and design within and beyond curriculum frameworks and guidelines.
3. Develop confidence in thinking about, planning, teaching and assessing primary art and design.

Art and design and young children

One of the real privileges of being a primary school teacher is that you encounter the fine detail of children exploring and examining, thinking about, investigating, challenging, representing and adding to their worlds. You are in a position to form close relationships between children and their ideas, as they navigate an undulating learning landscape. Primary school art and design sits comfortably in this landscape, as it encourages children to explore, to think about, to express, to communicate, to challenge, to investigate, to add to and to represent. Using a variety of stimulating materials and resources, art and design provides valuable opportunities to unlock interests and talent, and encourage creative endeavour.

For some children, the art and design experience is extremely positive and rewarding – they will enjoy the freedom and spontaneity of materials: stimulated by the flow of freshly mixed paint, excited by the flexibility of clay, or encouraged by the immediacy of a digital photograph. Some children will happily invent patterns, make up stories with drawings and words, cut sections from magazines to create imaginary creatures or see the potential in a cardboard box to become a home for a collection of toy ponies.

However, other children will appear less committed to art and design. They will appear to rush their drawings, moving to new and more interesting things; they will be uncomfortable using clay, finding that it gets down their nails and is cold and slimy to touch. Some children will be frustrated by the way paint does not always do as they would expect, turning muddy brown very quickly, or running down the page. When asked to invent something new, to create a design for a pop-up card, they will look to their neighbouring peer for support, adopting their ideas in their own plans.

Your role, as a teacher, is to reach this range of children with challenging, supportive, and interesting art and design lessons. This book sets out to help you achieve this.

Figure 0.1 Art and design is a powerful way of engaging children with their world

Question: *Do all children enjoy art?*
Response: Most children do enjoy the materials, processes and objects of art and design, and certainly children under 5 show very little reluctance towards exploring and investigating with these materials and processes. But as you will be aware, things change very dramatically during the primary school years: an 11-year-old is very different to a 4-year-old. Older children are increasingly conscious of their own likes and dislikes, their abilities and skills, and their willingness to take on board certain subjects or challenges. Art and design is no different – some children find art and design lessons frustrating, and would be far happier if there was less mess and greater certainty.

The question implies that enjoyment is equivalent to a positive learning experience. It is absolutely right that there should be some fun and enjoyment in school, but it is worth remembering that an appropriate teaching ambition would be to generate positive situations where 'learning is enjoyable'.

Question: *Are some children naturally talented at art and design?*
Response: Looking at the work of young children, there are certainly indications of some children producing work which looks more resolved or sophisticated. In some rare cases adult artists appear to have been prolific in their production of art as young children. Picasso is a well established example, painting and drawing with exceptional skill and talent at primary school age. He famously suggested that during his adult artistic life he was searching to make art more like that of a child. Whether these rare cases are formed from genetic differences, or are culturally learned behaviours, is very difficult to determine.

It is useful to consider the range of needs in your classroom and to share a commitment in the belief 'that everyone has the potential to work in artistic ways'. This will help you to keep an open mind about ability or talent, and resist the naming of some children as being 'good at art and design' and others as 'not so good'. Providing a variety of materials and varied activities will help pupils find ways of exploring ideas, impulses and feelings in successful ways, rather than being frustrated by more limited provision.

Teaching art and design to young children

You may find the prospect of teaching art and design to young children challenging yet exciting. Alternatively you may find the challenge slightly unnerving, troubled by the idea of having to manage a complicated and messy classroom as well as expose your own artistic abilities and awareness.

Much of this book is concerned with supporting your needs as a teacher of art and design and helping you to tackle the challenge, excitement or concern. One of the intentions of the book is to help you find solutions to diverse situations you might find yourself in, under the broad term of 'art and design'. This range will no doubt challenge you at times, and at other times you will feel more confident. The steps you take towards being a primary teacher involve you working out how you see yourself as a teacher, and for parts of this book, how you see yourself artistically.

One of the very real barriers to making progress as a primary school teacher of art and design can be found in the perception individuals have of their artistic or creative ability. Often this is understood and expressed through perceptions of drawing ability.

Question: *Do you need to be good at drawing to teach art and design?*
Response: This is a very common question. The ability to represent accurately the things observed or experienced is what shapes many definitions of drawing ability. This is a deeply rooted, culturally transmitted idea, initially born from an interest in perspective and accuracy, established in Western traditions of art during the Renaissance. Artists' drawn representations of objects, events, people and places, animals and environments, are often judged against the faithfulness of the representation: they look like the real things. However, drawing solutions presented by a range of artists and children tell us that drawing involves much more than accurate representation.

While drawing is a very useful and powerful feature of art and design, it also functions outside of art and design, serving as a representational and exploratory tool for many subject areas. As a result if perceptions and conceptions of drawing ability are holding back your ambition for teaching art and design, broadening your awareness of art and design practice may help.

Although teaching does require subject knowledge, understanding and skills, sometimes these will be exposed during lessons, for example, showing approaches to using tone to show three dimensions, or using line to represent positive and negative shape. There are many ways of illustrating and translating ideas for children other than through your own demonstrations. You can use examples from others, you could work alongside another adult or use children's examples, you could have an example ready prepared, or show a video clip of an artist working in a similar way. With experience you will build a repertoire of teaching interventions, not solely dependent on your own perceived artistic ability.

Question: *Is it possible to teach children to be artistic?*

Response: With good support, varied activities, challenging problems, group work, and interesting work on a variety of scales, you will be able to support learning in the practices and processes of artists: supporting creative, inventive and increasingly skilled responses.

To support children's artistic development you will need to embrace the idea that all children have the potential to work in this way, and that your support of this development will be important. Developing skills alongside opportunities to explore and investigate creative ideas will help support artistic inquiry. You will be able to observe children trying things out, testing out ideas, forming new ideas, arriving at solutions. You will also observe children running out of ideas, with limited skills and knowledge to develop and resolve their ideas. As a result, the planning, the teacher interventions and the observations and evaluations that you make will be increasingly important.

Planning, teaching and assessing art and design

This book will explore some of the complexities of teaching and learning as well as offer planning and assessment solutions. It is hoped that these will help you through the range of choices and decisions you face as a teacher as you prepare to teach; as you consider ways to share knowledge, provide experiences and develop skills, and as you consider ways of making sense of the development of children's understanding.

Question: *Is it possible to plan for creative art and design?*

Response: Planning and preparing to teach involves a whole series of decision-making steps and processes. In this sense planning plays as valid and important part of art and design as it does for other subjects. Lessons which are organised around teaching skills, or reinforcing knowledge and understanding, are more readily translated into learning intentions and objectives. Other lessons which aim to encourage more creative and inventive responses will be defined with learning intentions and objectives which sound more open, are more encouraging of different responses. However, in both cases the planning process will be detailed as you think through ways in which you will support initial ideas, stimulate interest and visual responses, how you will help develop ideas, and how you will help children bring their ideas together.

Question: *Is it possible to assess children's art and design?*

Response: There are advocates of art education who suggest that children's personal expressions through art and design are valid for the children who make them, and should not be assessed or monitored by a teacher. There is some mileage in this argument, but equally there is a suggestion that art and design responses deserve attention and review from teachers and children, similar to the ways in which other creative activities attract evaluation: story writing, musical composition or dramatic interpretations.

In this way, feedback can be given to pupils to develop work in various ways: working on different scales, with other combinations of materials, with greater control of techniques, with increased invention, or by applying knowledge of other artists and traditions. This approach to assessment will be sensitive to the intentions of pupils, while developing the discipline of art and design; its process, knowledge skills and values.

Identifying and supporting your needs

In your preparation to teach you will have received a wealth of information in the form of folders, lecture notes, reading packs, seminar handouts or web links. Some of this will be legislation, some guidance, frameworks, policies, strategies, pro-formas, ideas, initiatives, interventions, schemes or procedures. A real challenge for you is to take this information on board, sift through it and filter out what is sensible, and above all, to keep in mind yourself and the children you intend to work alongside.

As you do so there will be inevitable ebb and flow to your thoughts about teaching. Your teacher identity will emerge as you reflect, review and change, develop and consolidate. This book recognises the importance of your evolving identity and how it shapes your approaches to teaching. To support your changing needs we accept and acknowledge the process as dynamic, and encourage you to do the same.

This fluid and dynamic position encourages you to seek different support, at different times, or in different contexts. Above all it attempts to divert you from the temptation to 'fix' with one teacher type or identity. The book encourages you to avoid pinning yourself down, for example, as 'someone who is not creative' or 'someone who does not like art'. In this way you are encouraged to identify your needs in the contexts in which you find yourself. The case studies and examples used throughout illustrate this variety.

To help you make sense of this we have suggested three 'levels' at which you may find yourself working at different times, and in different situations, which form a *continuum of experience, needs, confidence and support.* We have described these levels as:

- **Introductory level:** probably with limited experience of art and design and as result seeks support and guidance to gain confidence;
- **Threshold level:** probably with some experience in art and design and a reasonable level of confidence, works with guidance and support but is willing to try things out and offer some new suggestions;
- **Beyond threshold level:** probably secure with many areas of art and design and happy to live with some risk and uncertainty, willing to try things out within existing plans and suggest new ideas.

It is an intention of this publication to appeal to, and support, this variety of experiences and confidence levels. The chapters acknowledge this variety and offer a range of solutions, expressed through the text and in practical and reflective tasks. However, responsibility lies in some part with the reader to acknowledge their own needs and interpret the publication's suggestions and guidance, prompts and cues, in appropriate ways.

For example, you may find yourself during a school placement supporting a lesson using digital cameras to identify, select and frame areas of pattern in the local environment, and you may consider yourself at an introductory level. However, on another occasion you may be working alongside a classroom assistant helping children develop texture by applying oil pastels to painted surfaces, this time describing yourself as being at a 'threshold level'. Different scenarios require different levels and types of support.

This shifting around is consistent with professional development models which promote a process of review and evaluation of teaching and of personal development. The Training and Development Agency (TDA): Professional Standards for Qualified Teacher Status (revised 2008) (TDA, 2008:6) confirm that intending teachers need to:

Reflect on and improve their practice and take responsibility for identifying and meeting their professional needs.

(Q7)

Have a creative and constructively critical approach towards innovation, being prepared to adapt their practice where benefits and improvements are identified.

(Q8)

PRACTICAL TASK PRACTICAL TASK PRACTICAL TASK PRACTICAL TASK PRACTICAL TASK

Having considered initial confidence levels against those described above you will be in a position to speculate about your own development and profile of action in terms of art and design. You will be able to continue refining and adjusting these considerations as you work through the book, but your initial observations can be supported by identifying areas of professional development identified by the *Professional Standards for Qualified Teacher Status* (QTS).

Refer to the QTS standards, keep your own level of confidence in mind, identify and review where areas for development are explored throughout the book.

Professional Standards for Qualified Teacher Status

The chapters and related activities will support your development towards the Professional Standards for Qualified Teacher Status. You will be able to develop your thinking about and approaches to:

- professional attributes;
- professional knowledge and understanding;
- professional skills.

Organisation

The case studies used throughout the book are based on teaching experiences and observations of young children working in primary art and design. They are used to shed light on the varied nature of art and design in schools, providing a context for your developing thoughts about how to plan, prepare, teach and assess primary art and design. They are also indicative of the spirit of the book which promotes a commitment to young children and their ideas, expressed through the materials of art and design.

The chapters are organised to:

- consider positive learning environments and experiences;
- identify appropriate learning for children;
- consider the teacher's role and responsibilities;
- identify curriculum guidelines and requirements;
- offer strategies for planning;
- address the complexities of assessment.

Chapter outlines

1   Art and design in primary schools: the current scene

This chapter provides an overview of current requirements in terms of curriculum frameworks and guidance, including the Early Years Foundation Stage (EYFS), and National Curriculum Key Stages 1 and 2. This chapter will help you identify these frameworks in relation to aims and rationales for primary school art and design, illustrating the diversity of activities that constitute an art and design education.

This chapter addresses the following Standards for QTS: **Q3, Q14, Q15**.

Key themes: statutory and non-statutory guidance; recent initiatives; creativity; aims; rationales; diversity; Early Years Foundation Stage; National Curriculum.

2   Art and design in the primary school: developing the scene, children as artists

The second chapter aims to help you develop your thinking about art and design education, beyond the requirements established in Chapter 1. It asks you to think a little more closely about the things children do when they are being creative and inventive, and to broaden your vision of what is considered as 'art and design'.

The chapter considers 'what creative artists do', making comparisons with what creative children do; they play with ideas, they seek out representations, reflect on them, adapt, modify and make changes. Your attention is then brought towards 'what creative teachers need to do', to support this more open version of art and design.

This chapter addresses the following Standards for QTS: **Q1, Q7, Q8, Q14**.

Key themes: creativity; invention; creative enquiry; artistry; aesthetic significance; active making.

3   Considering learners and learning: principles and practice

The chapter engages with ideas focused on the nature of learning from experience, the powerful nature of active learning, the idea of being intelligent through practical activity, and the need for reflection in all creative arts activity. Learning *through* art and design is explored, and key areas of learning in art and design are identified including concepts, processes, knowledge, skills and values with links to the EYFS and the National Curriculum.

This chapter addresses the following Standards for QTS: **Q1, Q2, Q10, Q18, Q19**.

Key themes: active and experiential learning; processes; knowledge; skills and values; reflection and evaluation; learning *in, through* and *about* art and design.

4 Knowledge and understanding: progression of experiences and processes

This chapter supports your understanding and experience of key areas of learning in art and design, knowledge of art experiences, processes and materials, visual qualities and artists, craftspeople and designers. Your awareness of progression and development will also be supported in this chapter.

This chapter addresses the following Standards for QTS: **Q14, Q15, Q27**.

Key themes: visual; tactile and spatial elements; experiences; processes; materials; progression; development; vocabulary; resources; ICT and digital media; artists; genres; styles; traditions.

5 Considering teachers and teaching: principles

This chapter will help you to consider your emerging identity as a trainee teacher, or early career teacher, and help establish your identity in a *continuum of experience, needs, confidence and support*.

The chapter introduces and develops three phases of experience: introductory level (limited experience and confidence); threshold level (some confidence and experience); and beyond threshold level (happy to live with risk and uncertainty). These phases or levels form an important part of your engagement with the book, as you evaluate your own needs, against your emerging and developing experiences, knowledge and understanding. They are used in this chapter to develop your understanding of the different approaches teachers take to teaching primary art and design.

This chapter addresses the following Standards for QTS: **Q1, Q7, Q8, Q10, Q14**.

Key themes: emerging identities; confidence; continuum; teaching and artistry; the artist teacher; teacher interventions; support and challenge; intervention and observation; professional understanding; traditions.

6 Considering teachers and teaching: practice

This chapter explores ways to support and challenge pupils, through the organisation of materials, resources, learning environment, and teacher interventions, towards purposeful and imaginative art and design. The chapter illustrates ways of supporting the processes embedded in the National Curriculum framework including the development of creative ideas using a 'productive toolbox'.

This chapter addresses the following Standards for QTS: **Q1, Q10, Q14, Q15, Q25**.

Key themes: teacher interventions; support and challenge; intervention and observation; professional understanding; decision making; choice taking.

7 Planning and preparing to teach: ideas into practice

This chapter pays particular attention to the process of planning and preparing to teach. It will illustrate the systematic process of planning, from initial ideas to completed long-term and medium-term plans, encouraging coverage, progression and interest. Short-term planning is presented to develop your thoughts towards structured and detailed plans to support learning within lessons.

This chapter addresses the following Standards for QTS: **Q3, Q14, Q15, Q22**.

Key themes: continuity; progression; development; experiences; processes; schemes of work; long-term, medium-term and short-term planning; objectives; lesson structure and content; evaluation and review.

8 Assessment, monitoring and feedback

This chapter supports your understanding and awareness of approaches to assessment, identifying assessment opportunities, making observations, providing support through feedback, monitoring, documenting and recording progress and achievement. References are made to the non-statutory National Curriculum level descriptors for art and design.

This chapter addresses the following Standards for QTS: **Q4, Q11, Q12, Q27, Q28**.

Key themes: assessment; evaluation; monitoring; reporting; feedback; development; documentation; progression.

9 Using sketchbooks in the primary school

This chapter develops your awareness of the possibilities and potential offered by using sketchbooks in the primary school. You will be able to identify the opportunities sketchbooks offer for children, to explore and develop work, investigate ideas in playful and creative ways, review and reflect on work. Sketchbooks are considered as an appropriate place to record feedback, supporting development and progress.

This chapter addresses the following Standards for QTS: **Q2, Q7, Q8, Q14, Q15**.

Key themes: investigation; documentation; research; enquiry; development; review; evaluation; children as artists; explore and store.

Following the content and themes outlined above, this book will support you in making the decisions which help children towards imaginative and purposeful experiences in primary art and design. It does this by broadening your awareness and knowledge of art and design, encouraging you to think about your teacher identity in flexible ways, by considering carefully the teaching interventions you can make, and by exploring the approaches you can take to planning and assessment.

REFERENCES REFERENCES **REFERENCES** REFERENCES **REFERENCES** REFERENCES

TDA (2008) *Professional Standards for Qualified Teacher Status and Requirements for Initial Teacher Training (revised 2008)*, available at http://www.tda.gov.uk/partners//ittstandards.aspx accessed July 2009.

1

Art and design in primary schools: the current scene

Chapter objectives

By the end of this chapter you will have:

- **broadened your awareness and understanding of primary school art and design;**
- **broadened your awareness and understanding of national frameworks and guidance;**
- **developed the connections you make between aims and rationales for art and design.**

This chapter addresses the following Standards for QTS: **Q3, Q14, Q15**.

Key themes: statutory and non-statutory guidance; recent initiatives; creativity; aims; rationales; diversity; Early Years Foundation Stage (EYFS); National Curriculum.

Introduction

This chapter provides an overview of the current requirements of frameworks and guidance for teaching art and design, including the Early Years Foundation Stage (DCSF, 2008), and National Curriculum Key Stages 1 and 2 (DfEE, 1999). It will help you identify these frameworks in relation to aims and rationales for primary school art and design, illustrating the diversity of activities that constitute an art and design education.

Children, schools and art and design

When we watch children play with materials, draw pictures or make things, there appears to be something special and meaningful about what they are doing. The drawings, paintings, models, constructions or scribbles may appear straightforward, and at times unsophisticated, yet there remains a fascination and interest, both from the perspectives of children and adults. We can stand and admire the freedom with which children use materials and tools to explore, explain, express, or recreate, invent, and imagine experiences of the world; the way children copy images and add new parts, creating wonderfully inventive characters; the way they play with toys to create new and exciting worlds, or tell stories of shopping trips with drawings, words and actions; the way they create elaborate worlds of fantasy from found and scrap materials.

Children involve themselves in this exploration and creation not to create art as such, but to make sense of increasingly complex worlds, to find ways of communicating and expressing ideas, feelings and impulses about their world and to invent new ones. It is other children, or more likely other adults, who introduce the term 'art' to children, sometimes calling it art and design, or art and craft, or just art. In schools or early years settings, dedicated areas are labelled and referred to as 'the art area' or 'the cutting and sticking table' or the 'junk modelling box', activities are called art and design, and children are described as 'doing art'. As a result, children get used to the idea that something exists which we call art and design. Adults show some interest in it. As experience in school develops lessons are named as art and design lessons, people are introduced as 'artists', examples of art are displayed via data projectors, and children begin to notice that some children in their class are good at being artists, while others are not. Teachers cut their artwork out, place words alongside it, turn it into funny shapes, and stick it to the classroom walls.

Your experience in schools will mean you are familiar with some of the things that go on in classrooms and in corridors, in school grounds and in school halls under the name of art and design, some led by children and some led by adults. It is worth remembering that the journey through schooling means children will encounter art and design in a number of different ways and value it for a number of different reasons.

- **Very young children explore the materials of art and design to see what the materials will do, how the materials react to their interventions.** Increasingly children explore how they can match materials to their experiences of the world – how dots on paper can be rain drops, parts of a recipe or the footsteps of a giant. They work out that lines on paper can be the legs of a rabbit or the journey to school, that circles become flowers, heads, hands, feet, eyes or wheels. Children will not call these creative activities art and design. Although some teachers or early years practitioners may be tempted to do so, others would see it as part of a continuum of tools and means with which to make meaning in an emerging world.
- **Children as young as 5 or 6 years old are introduced increasingly to lessons centred on art and design.** They learn about the materials of art and design, the artists who produce art and the ways they can talk about art and design. They will be asked to produce certain things and work with materials selected by teachers or teaching assistants. Increasingly they will be asked to do 'special' types of drawing, by looking closely and observing detail, to draw what they see rather than what they know. At other times, away from teachers or adults they will carry on making things up with pencils, felt pens, modelling materials, bits of cut up pictures, photographs and old pieces of wrapping paper. They will enjoy art works with subject matter which appeals to their interests.
- **As children's awareness of others develops, perhaps 6 to 8 years old, they begin to label some of their friends and peers as being 'good at art'.** They often base their judgements on the ability to draw cartoon characters, animals, imaginary creatures, flowers or colourful decorative patterns. Good artists will be those who can make things look like the real thing. Children will enjoy looking at narrative-based paintings and drawings, from a range of traditions and times; they will speculate about ideas in non-figurative works of art, enjoying visual qualities of colour, pattern and shape. They will make connections to other artists and the work in their classrooms, where teachers have introduced them to colour mixing and matching.
- **Some children become anxious about their ability to draw, between the ages of 9 and 11 and they may appear more reserved in their willingness to try new materials, or work on a large scale or in a group.** Children's ideas about what makes an artist and what makes a good artist may have become more sophisticated and the language used to describe them more developed. They will enjoy opportunities to explore and develop work in sketchbooks or other, more private places, working on recurring themes; telling stories with detailed action drawings, drawing things connected to their hobbies, horses, swimming or street dancing. Children will enjoy working alongside artists, admiring their expertise, creativity and skill. They may have ambitions of 'becoming an artist'.

REFLECTIVE TASK
REFLECTIVE TASK

Aesthetic development (suggested by Parsons (1987) adapted by Hickman 2005)	**Possible practical focus** (suggested by Hickman, 2005)
Stage one: sensuous response	Threshold skills
Stage two: representation	Perceptual training using a range of media
Stage three: expression	Exploration of expressive use of media; identity
Stage four: social and cultural awareness	Refining skills in the light of others' work

adapted from Hickman (2005, p44)

Figure 1.1 A possible developmental model for art and design learning

Refer to the 'practical focus' described in the right-hand column of Hickman's possible developmental model for art and design learning. Read the four stages described above left and make connections with Hickman's model. Reflect on how children move between different stages at different times and consider how this might impact on your approach to teaching.

Your school-based experiences will also tell you that different schools emphasise art and design in different ways. Some focus on skill development, others on personal expression and creativity, others focus on cross-curricular approaches to the arts, and others make use of practising artists. Some schools visit galleries regularly, some take on new initiatives through the inspiration of their art and design subject leaders. Other schools work closely with parents as helpers, or ask learning assistants to support art and design lessons. Some schools have art weeks, others art days, some combine art and design with design and technology. Some have strict guidelines for the presentation of work; others encourage children to produce displays. Some schools teach art and design lessons once a week throughout the year, others rotate with design and technology, one term art and design the next design and technology. Many schools have art and design subject leaders, some schools make use of sketchbooks. Some schools join in Big Draw events, others exhibit children's work; some keep assessment profiles and others document working processes with photographs and words.

PRACTICAL TASK PRACTICAL TASK PRACTICAL TASK PRACTICAL TASK PRACTICAL TASK

From the paragraph above extract the statements of what *some schools do* into a list. Organise and group these under the headings curriculum organisation, teaching approach, or resources.

From your school-based experience or from example schools taken from the internet (details can be found in school policies for art and design published on school websites), review a number of schools and their approaches to art and design and refer them to your list of statements. This will help you build a picture of what schools do in practice, and how they vary.

Aims and rationales for art and design education

For a number of reasons art and design continues to justify and explain its place in the curriculum. It does this through aims and rationales which are expressed in books, in school policies, by teachers, by subject associations, both in theory and in practice. You will notice this trend when you open most books about teaching primary art and design. Some time will be spent exploring the reasons why art and design is valuable to children, and why it deserves attention in an already busy school timetable.

Hickman (2005) reminds us that the *aims* of a teaching programme are the things we want to achieve, and the *rationales* are the reasons for wanting to achieve them. He suggests that schools tend to teach art and design to pupils to develop:

- understanding of their inner world, of feelings and imagination;
- understanding of the visual tactile and spatial world;
- judgements about the made environment;
- knowledge and understanding of art and design and culture;
- practical problem solving through the manipulation of materials;
- enhanced creativity through developing lateral thinking skills;
- inventiveness and risk taking.

(Hickman, 2005, p52)

It almost goes without saying that these things do not happen in every lesson, they do not happen in equal measure within a school, and different schools will identify certain areas as priority areas. However, these aims are useful to individuals and to social groups. They give children opportunities to explore personal and environmental issues; they offer chances to ask questions about why things are the way they are, to imagine new, fairer and more imaginative worlds; they develop transferable practical skills and they help children to make sense of the visual, spatial and tactile world around them. They encourage children to take the time to notice things which help make the world around them glisten: the intense colour of man-made fibres, the rich texture of freshly mixed plaster, the subtle colour palette of a sun-bleached landscape, the echo of sounds under a railway arch, or the softness of melting snow on an outstretched tongue.

In the National Curriculum (DfEE, 1999), the aims for art and design are expressed in terms of the subject's importance, suggesting art and design:

- stimulates creativity and imagination;
- provides visual, tactile and sensory experiences;
- provides unique ways of understanding and responding to the world;
- provides opportunities to communicate what is seen, felt or thought;
- encourages pupils to understand materials and processes;
- encourages pupils to explore and understand colour, line, pattern, texture, shape, tone and form;
- helps pupils make informed judgements;
- teaches pupils about artists, craftspeople and designers;
- helps pupils understand the role and function of art, craft and design in cultures;
- provides an opportunity to understand, appreciate and enjoy the arts.

(Adapted from the National Curriculum, DfEE, 1999, p116)

PRACTICAL TASK PRACTICAL TASK **PRACTICAL TASK** PRACTICAL TASK **PRACTICAL TASK**

Rewrite the list of National Curriculum statements on previous page. Make connections to Hickman's (2005, p52) statements where you can and write these next to the National Curriculum statements. Under each stage record three activities which would translate these aims into practical responses for the classroom. For example, 'encourages pupils to understand materials and processes', could involve children working in 2 and 3 dimensions, working with plastic, rigid and non-rigid materials, or combining different materials to create visual interest.

Curriculum requirements

Early Years Foundation Stage

CASE STUDY 1.1

On a blank piece of crisp white photocopying paper a 3-year-old boy stabs a broad-tipped marker pen; he does this repeatedly to the beat of 'pitter patter raindrops'. After a short while he shifts his chanted words to 'round and round the garden', and as he does so the marks he is making shift to large circular movements, some staying on the paper and some shifting to the table top. He stops to rub those on the table with his fingers, and then continues to pay close attention to his now red fingers.

A girl and a boy come in and out of the 'home corner' carrying trays of food – sausages made from rolled plasticine, and chips from torn paper. They tear more paper and offer 'tickets' to a small boy seated at a 'café table'. He pretends to drink tea and returns with the others to the home corner kitchen. Clutching their tickets they appear eager to prepare more food and drink from found materials and objects.

Under the supervision of an early years practitioner a small group of children cut colours that 'remind them' of 'Autumn' from selected magazine pages. They organise and stick the colours to pages of their book documenting their 'Crunchy Autumn Walk'. The boy with red fingers walks round the room, this time carrying a box of construction tools and wearing 'ear defenders' which he has crafted from an Alice band, some card, and two foil custard pie containers; he has 'jobs to do'.

The relationships between the materials and activities of art and design and learning, across the early years experience, are many and varied. Through the pursuit of personal interest and the interchange of ideas between themselves and others, children can be seen testing out a range of ideas. Art and design activities in themselves are there to be discovered and understood by children, as they learn how pens can be used to make 'footsteps', and paper to represent 'chips', or how scrap materials can become 'ear defenders'. But importantly the relationship between these materials, their properties and their use, to make meaning of the world through representational play should not be underestimated.

In Early Years Foundation Stage (EFYS) settings young children are supported in their understanding of areas of learning and development and early learning goals:

- personal, social and emotional development;
- communication, language and literacy;

- problem solving reasoning and numeracy;
- knowledge and understanding of the world;
- physical development;
- creative development.

Figure 1.2 Young children explore materials and ideas; they represent journeys in sand, explore routes through mark making, and capture experiences in collage

As the Early Years Foundation Stage Statutory Framework suggests:

> *None of these areas of Learning and Development can be delivered in isolation from the others. They are equally important and depend on each other to support a rounded approach to child development. All the areas must be delivered through planned, purposeful play, with a balance of adult-led and child-initiated activities.*
>
> (DCSF, 2008, p11)

However, close connections between what we know as art and design can be made to the area described as *creative development*:

> *Children's creativity must be extended by the provision of support for their curiosity, exploration and play. They must be provided with opportunities to explore and share their thoughts, ideas and feelings, for example, through a variety of art, music, movement, dance, imaginative and role-play activities, mathematics, and design and technology.*

By the end of the EYFS, most children will be able to:

- *explore different media and respond to a variety of sensory experiences, and engage in representational play;*
- *create simple representations of events, people and objects and engage in music making;*
- *try to capture experiences, using a variety of different media;*
- *respond in a variety of ways to what they see, hear, smell, touch and feel;*
- *express and communicate their ideas, thoughts and feelings by using a widening range of materials, suitable tools, imaginative and role play, movement, designing and making, and a variety of songs and musical instruments;*
- *explore colour, texture, shape, form and space in two and three dimensions;*
- *recognise and explore how sounds can be changed, sing simple songs from memory, recognise repeated sounds and sound patterns and match movements to music;*
- *use their imagination in art and design, music, dance, imaginative and role play and stories.*

(EYFS Statutory Framework, DCSF, 2008, p48)

Key Stage 1 and Key Stage 2

The National Curriculum 2000 (DfEE, 1999) is a revised version of the documented legislation first initiated as a part of the Education Reform Act 1988. Following fairly lengthy debate and discussion, the art and design attainment targets and programmes of study were developed to include a number of strands which encouraged engagement in both making and respond- ing to art and design. The programme of study is now revised to include both these aspects. This is an attempt to bring together a process of working in art and design, where making is supported by a process of increasingly knowledgeable review and evaluation.

It is worth remembering that in many ways any curriculum is an attempt to organise ideas and learning in a reasonably sensible way. A National Curriculum does this but on a huge scale, legislating for events in literally thousands of schools. It soon becomes clear that this sort of nationalised planning does not always serve the needs of individuals particularly well. Dividing and compartmentalising learning into subjects, while convenient, does little to reflect 'learning experiences'. Similarly, dividing each subject area into sections, or strands, while making a subject manageable, does not represent appropriately the interchange of ideas and processes evident in 'learning experiences'.

To overcome some of these tensions, we suggest you take on board the National Curriculum for art and design in a positive way, as a process-orientated model for learning, where children will move between the various processes at different times and for different reasons. This way, the orientation is towards learning, and learning experiences as opposed to what can be taught, monitored and measured. This is an attempt to maintain the integrity of children and their ideas, as well as the integrity of the subject.

You will need to familiarise yourself with the National Curriculum and the associated Qualification Curriculum Authority (QCA) scheme of work for art and design, not only to be compliant in your approach to teaching in schools, but to interpret the programme of study in a positive way.

The National Curriculum suggests learning in art and design includes:

- exploring *and* developing *ideas;*
- investigating *and* making *experiences, processes and materials;*
- evaluating *and* developing *work;*

To encourage a more considered approach to art and design these processes are supported by knowledge *and* understanding *of:*

1. *the* visual elements*: line, colour, tone, pattern, shape, space and form, and how these can be combined and organised for different purposes;*
2. materials *and* processes*: drawing, painting, printmaking, collage, digital media, textiles, and sculpture, and how these can be matched to ideas and intentions;*
3. artists, craftspeople *and* designers *working in different times and cultures, in a variety of genres, styles and traditions.*

(DfEE, 1999, p120)

REFLECTIVE TASK

Look at the EYFS goals for creative development and the Key Stage 1 and Key Stage 2 National Curriculum statements. How would you envisage managing a transition between these two approaches? How would you continue to promote creative development with Key Stages 1 or 2 children? Would you anticipate an age or phase where children are too young to take on board skill acquisition and development? Would you consider there to be barriers to introducing the work of artists, craftspeople and designers at particular key stages?

Between the programmes of study for Key Stage 1 and Key Stage 2 there are shifts in expectations and some indications of progression. For example, children move from 'recording' to 'selecting and recording', from 'investigate' to 'investigate and combine', from 'review' to 'compare'. These ideas of progressive activity are supported by the Qualification and Curriculum Authority (QCA) and their suggestions for progressive curriculum material within the National Curriculum framework. They offer suggestions for sequences of lessons and activities described and detailed in the QCA scheme of work for art and design. Some schools have taken these schemes as the basis for their own curriculum development, others have used them more or less unchanged and others pay only limited attention to the scheme. Any obligation to work with the schemes of work remains at the discretion of schools.

The schemes of work offer opportunities for children to work within the framework of the National Curriculum programme of study while developing progressive knowledge, skills and understanding. The QCA (2000) scheme of work is organised into three broad themes:

- self and experiences;
- natural and made objects;
- environments.

These themes are then presented as more specific projects which build on prior experience and learning:

Unit 1A Self-portrait	Unit 4B Take a seat
Unit 1B Investigating materials	Unit 4C Journeys
Unit 1C What is sculpture?	Unit 5A Objects and meanings
Unit 2B Mother Nature, designer	Unit 5B Containers
Unit 2C Can buildings speak?	Unit 5C Talking textiles
Unit 3A Portraying relationships	Unit 6A People in action
Unit 3B Investigating pattern	Unit 6B What a performance
Unit 3C Can we change places?	Unit 6C A sense of place
Unit 4A Viewpoints	Unit 9 Visiting a museum, gallery or site

(QCA, 2000, p25)

Key Stage 3: New Secondary Curriculum

Recent developments have led to a fairly major overhaul of the Key Stage 3 curriculum. Described as the *New Secondary Curriculum* (QCA, 2008b), the revised curriculum materials are based around aims to establish *successful learners, confident individuals* and *responsible citizens*. There is optimism that the revised legislation will encourage more links across the curriculum, respond to individual needs in more imaginative and sensitive ways, and promote learning through all aspects of school life, in classrooms, and beyond.

Developed with the help of subject organisations including the National Society for Education in Art and Design (NSEAD), the art and design material reflects a growing concern to marry skills and knowledge with more personally significant creative and inventive art and design work, suggesting a framework which includes:

Creativity
Imaginative ideas and responses
Exploring and experimenting with materials and processes
Taking risks and learning from mistakes

Competence
Processes: investigating, exploring, creating, developing, making, presenting, reflecting and reviewing
Skills: production, perception and discussion
Knowledge of techniques and materials

Cultural understanding
Engaging with a range of images, sounds and artefacts from a variety of different cultures
Understanding the role of the artist, performer, craftsperson or designer in a range of cultures, times and contexts

Critical understanding
Exploring sensory qualities of their own and others' work
Engaging with ideas and work of artists
Developing their own views and expressing reasoned judgements

Learning is supported by key skills and processes summarised as:

Explore and create

Understand and evaluate

(adapted from revised *New Secondary Curriculum*, QCA, 2008b)

REFLECTIVE TASK
REFLECTIVE TASK

Whether you are working with children in early years settings or in Key Stage 2, you will be increasingly involved in teaching art and design activity which attempts to build on creative intentions, with increased skills and knowledge. You will be encouraging children at all ages to reflect on, and to talk about their work and the work of others. Review and reflect on your own subject and pedagogical knowledge. Consider how this can be developed to support the variety of needs found in the classroom, and the demands associated with progression and development through the key stages.

Refer to the *continuum of experience, needs, confidence and support* detailed in the Introduction and developed in *Chapter 5: Considering teachers and teaching: principles*. Identify your awareness of the EYFS material and the National Curriculum, and describe yourself as either introductory, threshold or post-threshold, in relation to your knowledge and understanding of the organisation of these documents. Identify areas in the curriculum models where you will need to develop knowledge and understanding of:

- art and design experiences, processes and materials;
- visual elements;
- artists, craftspeople and designers.

Consider and reflect on your awareness of the following statements:

- Young children happily engage in art and design.
- They are told the thing they are engaged in is called art and design by others, usually adults.
- Children steadily get used to the idea that something exists called art and design.
- Schools and teachers perceive the benefits and aims of art and design in many different ways.
- Schools establish their own rationales expressed in policies and in practice.
- Schools organise their timetables, curriculum and resources in different ways.
- The experiences children have of art and design in schools will vary from one school to another.
- All schools will pay attention in some way to the National Curriculum or the Early Years Foundation Stage.
- Some schools pay close attention to the QCA schemes of work, others do not.
- Children need support in their art and design learning.

Having a good sense of what is required and suggested in national frameworks for teaching and learning in art and design will put you in a secure position as a teacher. You will gain confidence from this security, knowing how learning is described at different stages of primary school education, and gathering ideas of progression across the age phases. These aspects will be developed further and in more detail elsewhere in the book to provide developmental support for your teaching, planning and assessment in art and design.

From this position you are also encouraged to engage in some creative and imaginative thinking about what might be possible in primary art and design if we conceptualise children as 'artists'. This idea is explored and examined in *Chapter 2: Art and design in the primary school: developing the scene, children as artists*, which takes you beyond the frameworks, guidance, and expectations described in this chapter.

A SUMMARY OF **KEY POINTS**

This chapter has developed your awareness and understanding of:

> **primary art and design;**

> **art and design across age phases;**

> **aims, rationales and justifications for art and design;**

> **national frameworks, guidance, and expectations for art and design.**

MOVING *ON* > > > > > > MOVING *ON* > > > > > > MOVING *ON*

Next time you are in school apply your increased understanding and awareness of frameworks and guidance by observing and reflecting on the school's approach to planning and teaching art and design.

REFERENCES REFERENCES **REFERENCES** REFERENCES **REFERENCES** REFERENCES

DCSF (2008) *Early Years Foundation Stage Statutory Framework*. Nottingham: DCSF Publications.

DfEE (1999) *The National Curriculum*. London: HMSO.

Hickman, R (2005) *Why we make art and why it is taught*. Bristol: Intellect Books.

Parsons, M (1987) *How We Understand Art: a cognitive development account of aesthetic experience*. New York: Cambridge University Press.

QCA (2000) *Art and Design Teacher's Guide: scheme of work for Key Stages 1 and 2*. Sudbury: QCA.

QCA (2008a) *Early Years Foundation Stage Profile Handbook*. London: HMSO.

QCA (2008b) *New Secondary Curriculum for Key Stage 3*. Available at http://curriculum.qca.org.uk

2
Art and design in the primary school: developing the scene, children as artists

Chapter objectives

By the end of this chapter you will have:

- **broadened your awareness and understanding of creative activity;**
- **broadened your awareness of creative artistic activity;**
- **made connections between creative processes of artists and children;**
- **considered children as artists.**

This chapter addresses the following Standards for QTS: **Q1, Q7, Q8, Q14.**

Key themes: creativity; invention; creative enquiry; artistry; aesthetic significance; active making.

Introduction

The purpose of this chapter is to help you think a little more broadly about primary art and design, and extend the ideas presented in *Chapter 1: Art and design in primary schools: the current scene*. The chapter speculates about some of the possibilities for primary art and design which exist for young children beyond the frameworks of the National Curriculum (DfEE, 1999) and the Early Years Foundation Stage (EYFS) (DCSF and QCA, 2008a). It suggests that this is possible by thinking about 'children as artists'.

As you consider the things children do in primary schools during lessons, during wet break times, on the way to assembly or on the playground, you will begin to see children as creative and inventive people, with or without the added interventions of teachers. Children, like artists, play with ideas, they seek out representations, reflect on them, adapt, modify and make changes. They make images, objects, animations or poems, through common processes of investigation, enquiry, imagination and creation. Valuing these processes will help you take a step towards valuing individual creative ideas, and valuing children as artists.

The case study which threads through the opening part of this chapter is offered as an indication of the diverse activities children get up to during an everyday school encounter. They meet friends, play games, sing songs, eat snacks, walk on walls, talk about things, bring things in from home, share ideas, build things, take things home. Some of these things they do in the spirit of art and design where they investigate, enquire, imagine and create. The case study of The school day provides a flavour of this creative artistic activity.

CASE STUDY 2.1a

The school day 1

It is a damp start to the day, children huddle in small groups, with their parents and with their friends. A girl rummages around in her book bag, pulls out a colourful object and shows her 5-year-old friends. The object is made from combined lolly sticks, decorated with felt pen, constructed and held in the shape of a star with sticky tape; the girl names it as a 'wishstar'.

Despite the rain a group of Year 6 children skip with enthusiasm. As they do so they chant a repeated pattern of sounds and words, some discernible, others not. A number of younger children watch intently.

The entrance lobby to the school is bright and welcoming; messages declare the values and aims of the school, and a large display board shares work from the previous term's art week. The photographs show children of all ages, working in mixed age groupings, working on large and small scale productions: montage imagery combining drawings and magazine images, cut up and re-assembled toys, life size mod roc figures based on selected poses from gymnastics. A series of photographs depicts a carnival-style procession including decorative painted banners and spiralling willow and tissue structures.

REFLECTIVE TASK

As you read the case study think about your own experiences of primary schools, how they differ or what similarities they share. Think about which of the activities and events you would consider or describe as creative or artistic, and consider how you reach these conclusions.

Think about and identify the creative process involved in the actions and thoughts of children, as they identify, select, construct, combine, assemble, invent, and create.

Understanding creative activity

Attempting to pin down creative activity, with words or classifications, can begin to feel a little exasperating. The more you delve into ideas of creativity the more the concept feels as *slippery* as ever. However, it is useful to have a sense of key words, or developed vocabulary, which can be used to describe the actions of children and artists. In turn these actions can be allied to the creative artistic processes encountered in the case study.

The National Advisory Committee on Creative and Cultural Education (NACCCE) (1999) publication *All our futures: Creativity, culture and education* appeared during a period of government led drive to raise standards in mathematics and English; following the introduction of the Primary Numeracy and Literacy Strategies (DfEE, 1998). Although the initial impact of the NACCCE report was restricted by the emphasis on numeracy and literacy, it has since become a significant reference for those wishing to stimulate fresh ways of thinking about primary education.

In this important publication, creativity is considered as a mode for learning, which involves 'imaginative activity fashioned so as to produce outcomes that are both original and of value' (NACCCE, 1999, p29).

Using *imagination* involves:	Being *original* can be:
alternative outcomes the unconventional non-routine generating originality combining existing ideas re-interpreting making analogous relationships	individual: in relation to previous work relative: in relation to a peer group historic: it can be uniquely original
Pursuing *purposes* involves:	Judging *value* involves:
being actively engaged applied imagination being deliberate solving a problem changing from initial intentions	an evaluative mode of thought judgement and analysis individuals and groups trying out ideas critical thinking immediate response or longer periods of reflection

adapted from NACCCE, 1999, p29

Figure 2.1 Features of creativity

The document describes how it sees the relationship between *imagination*, *purpose*, *originality* and *value*, in both generative and evaluative terms. It goes on to suggest that 'helping young children to understand and manage this interaction between generative and evaluative thinking is a pivotal task of creative education' (NACCCE, 1999, p31).

The relationship between making (generative) and evaluation (evaluative) is echoed consistently in curriculum models for art and design, including the National Curriculum Council, Arts in Schools Project (NCC, 1990) and the current National Curriculum (DfEE, 1999). To promote these ways of thinking and working it is useful for teachers to be mindful of the complexity of the process. The relationship between making and evaluation does not necessarily follow a neat linear path, there will be notable periods of engagement; of *focus*, *withdrawal*, and *breakthrough* (NACCCE, 1999). In addition, the timescale can be stretched or, alternatively, things can happen quickly and suddenly.

CASE STUDY 2.1b

The school day 2

In the Reception class a group of children play in the sand area. They scoop out sand repeatedly, making a series of looping patterns which gradually change from 'tracks for cars' to 'tunnels for water'. Two boys sit together and build an unfeasibly tall tower from construction bricks. It topples over and they start again, this time securing the first bricks to a base. A group of children work alongside a classroom assistant, cutting and pasting regular shapes to create images of houses and homes, embellishing and decorating some areas to represent different textures.

A Year 1 class, discussing the Tudor period, are shown a series of paintings and asked to identify clues about the people within the images. One child suggests the painting is a portrait, probably of a king because he looks 'important and grand'; another adds that it might be a 'religious man'. A child sitting towards the edge of the group waves his hand and eagerly shares that he's 'had a portrait done ... with his dog'.

During wet playtime the school feels busier than ever; older children move around to engage in a variety of responsibilities, the windows steam up, and in almost every classroom children are drawing. Some are creating scenes of destruction with explosive noises as they draw, others invent patterns from a limited selection of pens, repeating colours and marks, others draw favourite things: ponies, dogs, planes and cars. Three boys cut out images of animals and birds from magazines, cut the heads from them and stick them to the bodies of football players: 'Look it's Parrotonaldo!' They laugh loudly.

PRACTICAL TASK PRACTICAL TASK **PRACTICAL TASK** PRACTICAL TASK **PRACTICAL TASK**

Write down in as much detail as possible all the things you have done in a day. Can you identify creative processes in the course of everyday events?

Think about a time when you were being creative. Did you have moments of focus, withdrawal and breakthrough?

Steers (2009), working from the ideas of Dewulf and Baille (1999), suggests a further useful summary of the creative process, involving four interlinked phases as shown in Figure 2.2.

- *Preparation* – in which the problem or question is defined, reformulated and redefined.
- *Generation* – moving beyond habitual pathways of thinking.
- *Incubation* – conscious planning and subconscious scanning of the problem or idea, often following a period of relaxed attention.
- *Verification* – where ideas are analysed, clustered and evaluated, followed by detailed planning and implementation.

(Steers (2009) after Dewulf and Baille (1999))

Figure 2.2 Creative processes

To summarise these ideas, we can suggest that creative activity involves:

imagination, originality, purpose and value.

We can identify the process as involving phases of:

preparation, generation, incubation and verification.

We realise that the procedure is neither clear cut or straightforward, but involves:

focus, withdrawal and breakthrough.

While we accept the complexity of these terms, but in no way suggest them as definitive accounts for creative activity, they remain useful starting points as we consider what children and artists do. We can begin to consider and develop our understanding of the productive processes children and artists share, involving physical, intellectual and emotional acts. Among other things they:

accumulate	sequence	adapt	combine
select	modify	edit	juxtapose
sort	change	repeat	embellish

By doing so they become engaged in what we can describe as playful investigation. It is during such moments that children may well immerse themselves in the habits of artists; they will be playful, inventive and creative with ideas, feelings, impulses and materials. Many of these processes can be seen across the curriculum and are not exclusive to the arts or to artists. They are echoed in subjects as apparently diverse as science, dance, music or history. Thinking in terms of these 'processes' will help keep your mind open to the playful possibilities of school-based activities. This is important for the creative development of children, particularly when 'subjects' tend to shape and dominate both timetables and teaching.

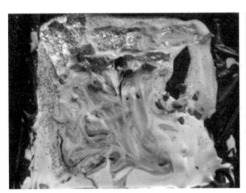

Figure 2.3 Children act in artistic ways, they explore, select, combine, assemble and present; they are playful and disciplined

What do creative children do?

Children do all sorts of things in their homes, on the way to school, in classrooms, and in the playground which we can consider as being creative. They:

make up songs	turn sticks into weapons	invent words
tell jokes	create secret routes	colour things in
draw pictures	invent games	imagine journeys

From this short initial list you will get a feel for the creative processes children engage with. They act in ways which are:

playful, imaginative, personal, cultural, emergent, open, flexible, disciplined, skilful, thoughtful, intelligent, engaging, purposeful, practical, inventive, interesting, expressive.

They involve themselves in creative productive processes, where they:

identify, select, construct, combine, assemble, invent, create, explore, develop, investigate, enquire, imagine, represent, reflect, evaluate, present, adapt, modify.

CASE STUDY 2.2

The school day 3

A group of girls point and talk while eating crisps and apples. They are in the main linking corridor looking at a display of 'bags', stitched and embellished by a Year 3 class and seem impressed by colour and detail. Further along the corridor they are attracted to a presentation of 'colour and paint', reflecting the bold use of colour found in the work of British-born painter David Hockney.

The afternoon arrives and two adjacent Year 4 classes join together for an art lesson, billed as the 'start of an exciting project'. Building on work in geography where they looked at contrasting environments, the children are encouraged to think about themselves as explorers on an imaginary island. Their first task is to document what they can see and find; using their previous geographical knowledge. They are encouraged to think about climate, habitat and population. Working in groups the children record their ideas on large sheets of paper in the form of words. On a second large sheet of paper, with broad marker pens the children begin to draw their imaginary islands. They add harbours, churches, farms, forests, water sources, hills, bridges, roads and villages. Very soon the classroom is awash with invention and intrigue, about the habits and pastimes of these new locations.

Walking home from school two boys ask if they can visit the park. While they are playing they begin to act out some of the island adventures. At the edge of the park, under a large tree, two girls build 'nests' for pebbles with carefully selected and arranged sticks and grasses. Back at home the lolly sticks are labelled with a 10p price label and placed on a table as part of a shopping game.

PRACTICAL TASK PRACTICAL TASK PRACTICAL TASK PRACTICAL TASK PRACTICAL TASK

Make a list of all things children might do in a primary school which share some of the characteristics of creative art and design activity. Does this surprise you in any way? Perhaps the range of materials and activities is much broader than you had thought before? Does the list of activities you describe reflect different phases of primary education?

Children and creative artistic activity: personal and social development

Before we get too carried away with considering everything we do as being artistic, and everything creative being worthwhile, it will be useful to pause and consider the justifications of creative artistic activity in educational terms.

Historically, teachers, governments and theorists have offered a number of varied justifications (see *Chapter 1: Art and design in primary schools: the current scene*) for the creative and artistic activities of children. Justifications are sometimes overheard in conversations between staff, or they may exist more formally, documented in school policies. For example, policies may include the claim that: 'art and design is an opportunity for children to explore creative forms of expression, where personal ideas and growth are encouraged'. Often justifications rest on the belief that creative activity is 'good for individuals'. In other situations a sense of social responsibility may be evident in policy material, where 'art and design encourages individuals to listen to and value the ideas of others; to share ideas in a community that embraces difference'. This combination of values is a recurring theme in debates about the value of creative art and design education. Where at first the individual and society may appear in opposition, with further thought they can be considered co-dependent and intertwined.

Creative artistic activity and personal development

Personal development through creative activity has been a suggested claim of many art educators. A series of developments in art and design education through the twentieth century often hinged on debate around the centrality of the child, their creative expression, and their wellbeing, as outcomes of an education in art and design.

In the publication *Creative and mental growth*, first published in 1947 and now reprinted in its eighth edition, Viktor Lowenfeld influenced, and continues to influence, the ways in which we think about children and their art. Much of his writing focuses on the significance, the development and the meaning of children's creative art activities. Lowenfeld presents a view of children's art activity as being spontaneous and personal, and inevitably questions how teachers can encourage and preserve such creative expression. His conviction remains that creative art and design activities provide opportunities for personal, mental and emotional development:

> Art is a dynamic and unifying activity, with great potential for the education of our children. The process of drawing, painting or constructing is a complex one in which the child brings together diverse elements of his experience to make a new and meaningful whole. In the process of selecting, interpreting, and reforming these elements, he has given us more than a picture or a sculpture; he has given us a part of himself: how he thinks, how he feels, and how he sees.
>
> (Lowenfeld, 1982, p3)

You will be able to identify Lowenfeld's concern for the individual, and the sense that art provides an opportunity for the expression of ideas, impulses and feelings; the promotion of unique responses, through which children 'reveal themselves'.

REFLECTIVE TASK

Think back to when you were at school, or as a student involved in creative activity. Did you get a sense, possibly from the teacher, the way they taught or the things they said, that you were being encouraged to develop as a person, through the expression of thoughts and feelings? Was there a sense that your freedom of expression needed to fit alongside, or added to, a community spirit? Can you identify any tensions with this relationship, between the promotion of the individual and civic responsibility?

Creative artistic activity and social development

In addition to the ideas of personal development through creative activities there are those who advocate a more public spirited account, highlighting social contributions. Perhaps the most obvious, although slightly less egalitarian, are the arguments that promote creative contributions in economic terms. They realise the potential in creative individuals to add to the market economy. The creative industries themselves are often referred to as generating an output towards £100 billion, almost 8% of the United Kingdom's economy (Department for Culture Media and Sport (DCMS), 2006 p5).

Beyond the economic argument there are those who claim social renewal through creative activity. According to Lowenfeld, a positive educational system, with creative values, will do much to realign the person, not only with their self, but with increased identification of others, through a shared understanding of the creative process. In other words, if a class of children is engaged in creative activity they share a creative bond which unifies them as a group.

Bentley (2005) furthers the argument for creative activity and social engagement. He considers creative activity as being crucial in the re-emergence of the individual, within its society and forms of governance:

> *It would be easy to posit creativity as an ideal, an answer to the challenges of today's society. It would likewise be easy to fall into the trap of assuming that creativity can be 'taught'. Unfortunately, there is no formula – and can be no syllabus – for creativity.*
>
> *What we can, however, do is develop the conditions within which it can flourish and the challenges to which it can respond. Creativity is more an outlook that can be encouraged, a way of identifying and approaching problems with innovation, confidence, and anticipation. As such, it emerges as a crucial means by which the individual can engage with his or her wider communities.*
>
> (Bentley, 2005, p10)

Bentley captures this moment of authentic engagement with the world that children seem to exhibit through their work, the kind of moments we have seen in the case study, The school day. He suggests that:

> *[c]hildren's art is thus not solely about learning how to draw, paint, sculpt or work in any other media. To see the child as producing 'art' is to think of him or her as a conscious participant in what is essentially an adult process. Far better, instead, to think of what the child is getting out of its creative engagement and what, consequently, the effect might be as the child grows up.*
>
> (Bentley, 2005, p6)

The significance of children making nests for pebbles, inventing humorous characters from birds and football players, or stitching repeated patterns to felt bags, should not be underestimated. Hickman describes these encounters and activities as *aesthetic significance* and that the makers appear to have an 'urge to create (such) aesthetic significance' (Hickman, 2005, p133). That urge can be captured and enhanced by teachers in a way that helps keep learning and teaching fresh and meaningful. As Anthony Gormley (cited in Hickman, 2005) suggests,

> *[i]n education, the experience of making through art emancipates the individual from the already-made world by re-enforcing her as a maker ... the art room can become a zone dedicated to the exercise of curiosity ... allowing her to become an active maker of living culture and not just a consumer.*
>
> (Gormley, in Hickman, 2005, p7)

REFLECTIVE TASK

These claims for art and design education, and the power of creative action, can sometimes sound a little overstated. The claims are certainly big. However, think about a situation where a creative approach has given the group a sense of identity and helped forge it together. Has there been a creative spirit amongst you which has contributed to a positive learning experience? You might equally recall a time when creative activity was the last thing you wanted to engage in and you found it frustrating.

Creative artists

What do creative artists do?

Keeping in mind the ideas discussed so far in the chapter, you are now encouraged to make connections to the things that creative artists do. The Introduction suggested that artists are:

imaginative	focused	curious	inventive
perceptive	determined	developmental	motivational
reflective	independent	practical	mediawise
collaborative	playful	environmental	thoughtful

While the content of creative artists' work may well look, sound, or feel very different, it tends to revolve around ideas that develop and evolve within and beyond particular traditions; landscape, the human figure, still life, events and narrative-based ideas and the abstract (Taylor, 1999).

In their explorations and representations, creative artists almost always play around with ideas and materials through processes of manipulation, transformation, construction, reshaping or translation. They:

identify, select, construct, combine, assemble, invent, create, explore, develop, investigate, enquire, imagine, represent, reflect, evaluate, present, adapt, modify.

They do so by playing with materials and ideas using a range of productive devices, amongst other things they:

accumulate	sequence	adapt	combine
select	modify	edit	juxtapose
sort	change	repeat	embellish

These processes of enquiry echo the creative processes of children and are a powerful way of recognising children as creative artists.

Who is an artist?

In this enquiry the use of the term 'artists' refers to a spectrum of artists, craftspeople and designers. This encompasses a broad range of creative practitioners that work in the creative arts industry. Some possibilities are listed on page 31.

What do creative artists do?

Who: Dave Gibbons

Artistic practice: Photographer

Training: Winchester School of Art 1996–2000

Artistic traditions: Photography, narrative, landscape, figure

Related artists: David Levinthal, Ettiene Clement, Sian Bonnell

Dave Gibbons is principally a photographer. He works extensively in film and digital media, to produce images, often as a series, and often thematically conceived. The subject matter of his work varies, as do his methods of recording and developing work. He may come across a ready made scene, explore an interesting found object, notice something on a cycling journey to work, or follow his instinct for combining and placing unusual things together. The results include photographs of toy figures, carefully placed in constructed environments, distorted and diffracted representations of locations, and collections of images representing the life and times of football.

Creative Art & Design Process	IMAGINATIVE	PURPOSEFUL	VALUABLE
	Preparation	Generation	Incubation	Verification
	FOCUS	WITHDRAWAL	BREAKTHROUGH

Creative artists can almost always play around with ideas and materials through processes of manipulation, transformation, construction, reshaping or translation. they:

Identify, Construct, Combine, Assemble, Invent, Create, Explore, Develop, Investigate, Enquire, Imagine, Represent, Evaluate, Present, Adapt, Modify

Creative artists can be:

Imaginative	Focused	Mediawise	Inventive
Perceptive	Determined	Developmental	Playful
Reflective	Independent	Motivational	Curious
Collaborative	Thoughtful	Environmental	Practical

Following a career as a carpet fitters, Dave turned his full attention to being an artist. The unusual amount of time spent at ground level incubated an idea for low level panoramic images. A breakthrough for this work came one frosty winter morning: a local playing field, a heavy hoar frost, and, by coincidence, a toy football player in his pocket. A series of 'figures' in panoramic spaces followed.

Encounters

For this series of images Dave has modified and adapted toy figures and environments to create playful and thought provoking encounters. By placing objects together in playful and imaginative ways, stories and narratives begin to unfold. In many of the images Dave manipulates the scenes, both optically and digitally, to enhance visual qualities of space, colour and light. Perhaps of most significance is his sustained exploration of isolation and scale.

Football

As an important part of Dave's life, football has proved a motivation for a number of photographic adventures, recording, documenting, and accumulating memories from footballing events, spaces and objects. Dave captures and intensifies these moments through careful selection and editing.

Amongst other things creative artists do:

Accumulate	Sequence	Arrange	Wrap
Select	Layer	Edit	Juxtapose
Sort	Change	Repeat	Embellish

Figure 2.4 What do creative artists do?

Academic researcher	Garden designer	Sculptor
Animator	Graphic designer	Sound recordist
Archivist	Interior designer	Sign writer
Architect	Jewellery designer	Silversmith
Book illustrator	Knitting designer	Stage designer
Bookmaker	Model maker	Stained glass maker
Ceramicist	Mosaic designer	Stone mason
Conservationist	Muralist	Tattooist
Costume designer	Packaging designer	Teacher
Curator	Painter	Technical illustrator
Fashion designer	Photographer	Textile designer
Film maker	Potter	Visual artist
Gallery educationalist	Printer	Weaver

It is this population of the art world that the National Curriculum refers to when it suggests children develop knowledge and understanding of a range of artists, craftspeople and designers. An artist is an individual who creates and realises their ideas and philosophies through using the materials of their choice. This can be produced for self-expression, commercial purpose, or social comment. The work might be viewed publicly or not, it might be produced for a client to a brief, or to be exhibited and available for sale. Another scenario is that a practitioner produces artwork for a market in order to be commercially viable. Across this diverse range of contexts they will share creative qualities.

PRACTICAL TASK PRACTICAL TASK **PRACTICAL TASK** PRACTICAL TASK **PRACTICAL TASK**

Visit www.artisancam.org.uk and follow the links to view the work and working processes of the following artists:

- Chun Chao Chiu

- Maddi Nicholson

- Rebecca Chesney

As you watch the videos and refer to the images consider the key points of the chapter, what are the artists' characteristics: are they sculptors, land artists, jewellery makers? What creative processes do the artists share, what differences are evident, are there periods of incubation or breakthrough, focus or withdrawal?

Who counts as an artist?

Those working in art, craft and design are motivated to create aesthetic representations of their thinking that contain personal values, imagination and beliefs, what Hickman (2005) describes as 'aesthetic significance'. Each artist is an individual and each piece of their work is unique. Their motivation and purpose for creation will be wrapped in its own aesthetic vision. The work may make reference to personal, natural, and social considerations, alongside the creative abilities of the artist. The actual creative process they travel through to arrive at their art work goes through a series of steps and stages. Generally this could be thought of as following a process from initial thoughts/concept, research, investigation, exploration and experimentation with materials and form, review and development, to creation and realisation of work and sale/exhibition. An artist might step in at any point of this process and use all or some of these steps.

During the process an artist may go through a creative journey of *incubation, breakthrough* and *withdrawal* to arrive at an art piece. The process for producing art requires that artists develop a form of expression to embody their perceptions, their observations; their ideas, impulses and feelings.

Chidren as artists

Recent developments in secondary school education have acknowledged this way of thinking about children and artists. The *New Secondary Curriculum for Key Stage 3* suggests that children:

> *learn to think and act as artists, craftspeople and designers, working creatively and intelligently. They develop an appreciation of art, craft and design, and its role in the creative and cultural industries that enrich their lives.*

> (QCA, 2008b)

While the purpose of an inclusive primary art and design education is not primarily concerned with creating artists as such, the relationship to artistic practice and the enquiry made by children into ideas, feelings, impulses and materials is very similar. Children want to explore, to find things out, they want to discover, challenge, stimulate and enjoy, they want to see what happens when or if or how or why. Engaging children in this level of creative activity gives rise to individuals who are active in the creation and representation of their worlds; they create and engage with Hickman's (2005) 'aesthetic significance' and Gormley's (2005 in Hickman, 2005) 'curiosity'.

Perhaps one of the qualities and characteristics we sometimes overlook in an artist's pursuit of aesthetic significance, is the drive and determination required to achieve it. Dave Gibbons for example, will spend hours, usually alone working playfully and systematically, with found objects and toys, changing them in small yet significant ways. The implication for this, and other claims of this chapter, is how to translate these ideas to the classroom. The possibility of enabling ways of working that are playful and inventive, time-consuming and sometimes repetitive has implications for resources, teaching, the curriculum, assessment and accountability.

Further chapters will address these concerns and ideas.

PRACTICAL TASK PRACTICAL TASK PRACTICAL TASK PRACTICAL TASK PRACTICAL TASK

Refer to the *continuum of experience, needs, confidence and support* detailed in the Introduction, and developed in *Chapter 5: Considering teachers and teaching: principles*, and identify the level at which you think you are willing to take on the ideas suggested in this chapter:

Introductory level: You may have doubts about the concept of children as artists or need more convincing that there is 'room' in primary schools to think about children in this way. Reflect on the ideas summarised below, and try to remain open-minded when you visit a primary school. Pay particular attention to the things going on at the 'edges' of school life, outside of lessons, in corridors and in playgrounds and see if any of the language associated with children as creative artists can be used to analyse what you see.

Threshold level: you may have some reservations but on the whole are happy to take on board the general principles suggested in the chapter. When you next visit a school draw up a chart similar to Figure 2.4 and complete the figure not for an 'artist' but for children. Describe their activity and make connections to the creative process words.

Post-threshold level: From your own experiences you will be able to make connections to the ideas developed in this chapter. You will be excited about considering children in such creative ways, for their sense of individual growth and the ways they can engage critically with their communities. Re-work Figure 2.4 with an example of your own creative arts practice and use the process words to analyse your own creative activity.

All levels: As you consider the ideas in the chapter, you may make connections to how children work and how you work. Sometimes you might spend longer on a period of initial thoughts, whereas another time you may arrive at final pieces of work more quickly. From your observations of children, you will see how they move between ideas and materials, shifting contexts and environments. What might begin life as an idea, drawn during wet play, may well have the potential to become a short animation. With the appropriate level of support children can develop and sustain ideas over long and short periods of time; they can act and think as artists.

A SUMMARY OF **KEY POINTS**

> **Creative activities are tricky to fully pin down.**

> **Creative activities appear to share characteristics, phases and processes.**

> **The range of outcomes of creative activities is diverse.**

> **Children engage in creative processes similar to those of artists.**

> **Creative activities contribute to community and personal growth.**

> **Children can be considered as creative artists.**

MOVING *ON* > > > > > > MOVING *ON* > > > > > > MOVING *ON*

Go out of your way to involve yourself in some artistic and creative activities, read a novel, write a poem, watch a film, look up at buildings, play an instrument, sew something together, knit, or bake a cake. Think about the processes which bond this diverse range together.

REFERENCES REFERENCES **REFERENCES** REFERENCES **REFERENCES** REFERENCES

Bentley, T (2005) *So Giotto drew on rock: Children's right to art and everyday democracy*. Available at: www.demos.co.uk/publications/sogiottodrewonrocks (accessed 02/05/09).

DCSF (2008) *Early Years Foundation Stage Statutory Framework*. Nottingham: DCSF Publications.

DCMS (2006) *Developing Entrepreneurship for the Creative Industries: making the case for public investment*, available at http://www.culture.gov.uk/images/publications/PublicInvestment.pdf accessed July 2009.

Dewulf, S and Baille, C (1999) *How to Foster Creativity*. London: DfEE.

DfEE (1999) *The National Curriculum*. London: HMSO.

Hickman, R (2005) *Why we make art and why it is taught*. Bristol: Intellect Books.

Lowenfeld, V and Brittain, WL (1982) *Creative and mental growth*. New York: Macmillan (first published 1947).

Meager, N (2006) *Creativity and culture: Art projects for primary schools*. Corsham: NSEAD.

NACCCE (1999) *All our futures: Creativity, culture and education.* Report from the National Advisory Committee on Creative and Cultural Education, to the Secretaries of State for Education and

Employment, and Culture, Media and Sport, DfEE.

National Curriculum Council (NCC) (1990) *The arts 5–16: Practice and innovation,* Harlow: Oliver and Boyd.

QCA (2008a) *Early Years Foundation Stage Profile handbook.* London: HMSO.

QCA (2008b) *New Secondary Curriculum for Key Stage 3.* Available at: http://curriculum.qca.org.uk

Steers (2009) Creativity: Delusions, Realities, Opportunities and Challenges. *International Journal of Art and Design Education*, 28(2), pp126–138, 2009.

Taylor, R (1999) *Understanding and investigating art: bringing the National Gallery into the art room.* London: Hodder & Stoughton.

www.artisancam.org.uk

FURTHER READING FURTHER READING **FURTHER READING** FURTHER READING

Barnes, R (2006) *Teaching art to young children 4–9*, 2nd edn. Abingdon: RoutledgeFalmer (Chapter 14).

Bowden, J (2006) *The primary art and design subject leaders handbook.* Corsham: NSEAD.

Meager, N (2006) *Creativity and culture: Art projects for primary schools.* Corsham: NSEAD.

Wilson, A (ed) (2005) *Creativity in primary education.* Exeter: Learning Matters.

3
Considering learners and learning: principles and practice

Chapter objectives

By the end of this chapter you will have:

- **developed your understanding of children as learners in art and design;**
- **developed your understanding of the nature of learning experiences in art and design;**
- **developed your understanding of what children learn from art and design experiences.**

This chapter addresses the following Standards for QTS: **Q1, Q2, Q10, Q18, Q19**.

Key themes: active and experiential learning; processes; knowledge; skills and values; reflection and evaluation; learning *in, through* and *about* art and design.

Introduction

This chapter aims to identify how children learn from art and design experiences, and the ways in which teachers and educators attempt to describe that learning. It sees children in a developmental continuum from Early Years to early Key Stage 3. The chapter suggests that children: learn *processes* associated with art and design (they investigate, make, present, review, adapt, develop); develop *knowledge* (of materials and techniques: painting, drawing, printmaking, 3D work, textiles, lens-based media; of artists, genres, styles and traditions; of visual, spatial and tactile qualities: colour, line, shape, pattern, tone, texture, surface, shape, form and space); they develop *skills* (productive, perceptive and discursive) and they explore *values*.

In addition, children learn things *through* engaging with art and design. They learn more about the Tudors by building models of houses, they explore locations and maps, developing geographical knowledge, they learn a little more about themselves and each other by sharing ideas, listening to others, being creative or having an opinion about an artist's work.

In order to help them learn these things, and possibly more, art and design lessons centre upon a commitment to experiences that are active, personal, and reflective. In this way children can be encouraged to develop and refine their own processes, knowledge, skills and values in ways which reflect their creative, personal and cultural needs. This chapter will help you think a little more about this approach to learning, as well as giving you a secure sense of how to describe practical activities in valid educational terms.

Children and learning

Experience and learning

The world is a complicated place, and learning about that world is a complex and lengthy process. By involving children in an active and interesting art and design education you will be able to help them make a little more sense of the experienced world and their evolving place in it, by manipulating materials, by playing with ideas, and through the exploration of impulses, feelings and emotions. In many ways this is what all education hopes to do, and to achieve this it organises learning in formal places called schools, through intertwined structures called curricula, in things called lessons, and via the relationships established with others. In these situations young people share, and are involved in, experiences. Through these experiences children test out existing ideas, they take on board emerging ideas, they begin to develop understanding.

In these learning situations, children use their imagination to transform knowledge and understanding. Through the increasingly skilful manipulation of materials and resources they explore ideas by playing with vocabulary, and test out understanding via sensory examination and physical experience. As a result of this process, children begin to demonstrate cognition, and increasingly sophisticated conceptual awareness. This experiential approach to learning is not, by any means, exclusive to art and design. However, many art and design educators have promoted the importance of this developmental and active approach. Prentice (2003) suggests that 'central to learning in art is the concept of *lived experience*. Understanding is created and recreated through a process of construction and reconstruction of events (not as result of climbing another rung of a ladder)' (Prentice, 2003, p37).

In an active and experiential learning encounter children begin to understand things through physical, emotional and mental processes of enquiry. Children learn through their senses. They benefit from teaching encounters and curriculum materials which provide opportunities to represent their learning through a similar sensory range. For example, ideas can be explored and examined, presented and represented, through the body, in the form of dance, through words and sounds, through visual, tactile and spatial means. In this way, learning and teaching could readily involve taking photographs, producing a dance sequence, recording found sounds, or sculpting from reclaimed objects. This approach to considering learning and learners asks you to consider the whole learner, and to value their holistic representations of understanding. 'Learning of this transformational kind involves the whole person, it embraces in a holistic way, thinking and feeling, perceiving and doing' (Prentice, 2003. p37).

To make best use of this holistic approach to thinking about learning, you may have to take something of a leap of faith towards *the things that can be considered as evidence of learning*. Perhaps more than that, to accept that in themselves *things* embody learning. The *things* may include physical gestures, sounds, movements, drawings, painterly actions, sewn threads, sequenced imagery, or embellished vessels. This is not easy, and in a world where we try to pin things down in fairly ordered rationalised ways, it asks you to live with a 'sense of learning' in the physical actions of children, in the objects they produce, and in their expressions of emotion; these *are learning* and *they make contributions to further learning.*

Through practical activity, discussion and evaluation, art and design lessons give children the opportunity to transform understanding, knowledge and skills into more concrete images and artefacts. While this model of learning relies heavily on the transformative, experiential and personal, it also requires the active commitment of a teacher to support the development of learning. Children, like adults, need time and space to sustain and develop ideas, as they work things out in clay, on paper or through paint. As a result, the drawing solutions children produce, the clay animals they model, or the photographs they compose, embody knowledge, they are evidence of children's thinking and understanding. It could be argued that the role of an art and design education is to help children in the making of these visual, spatial or tactile statements. To do so requires an education that not only provides skills and knowledge, but encourages children to think in visual, spatial or tactile ways, to develop their visual literacy, both in terms of production and appraisal. 'To function with confidence and competence in the field of art and design learners from their earliest age should be initiated into the various codes and conventions through which visual modes of communication and expression in diverse cultural contexts are made possible' (Prentice, 2003, p37). By making art, by looking at art, by talking about it, children begin to see how others have made sense of complex worlds, and how they fit into those worlds.

REFLECTIVE TASK

Think about your experiences of learning. It might be a sport or a song on the guitar, how to play a computer game, or how to operate a new washing machine. Consider how you bring prior knowledge and experience to these situations in an attempt to work things out. Consider how you then draw on other people to build and develop your understanding. It might be a phone call to your mum or a friend or you might look something up in an online manual, or find out from a forum. Try to recall that feeling or sense of understanding, and how difficult it may be to pin it down.

As you move towards planning, preparing, teaching and assessing art and design, it will be useful to keep in mind the process of learning described, albeit briefly, above. By doing so you will be able to consider the complexities of learning encounters which:

- recognise the importance of active and personal experience;
- encourage playing around with 'understanding' through a range of materials and processes;
- value the objects and images children make as evidence of thinking and learning;
- encourage the consolidation of thinking and learning over periods of time;
- establish the role of other adults and the learning environment in promoting visual, tactile and spatial learning.

PRACTICAL TASK PRACTICAL TASK PRACTICAL TASK PRACTICAL TASK PRACTICAL TASK

Keep a record for a week of how you learn things through combinations of your mind, body, and emotions, and through what means you express your understanding. It could be by scoring a try in a game of rugby, remembering a name in a quiz, or compiling a digital musical play list for a friend.

Learning from practical activity and from others

To think skilfully is an act of intelligence, and to modulate technique so that it serves one's purpose requires sensitivity to nuanced qualities.

(Eisner, 2002, p80)

One of the exciting things about teaching and learning in art and design is the exploration of materials through practical activity. At times art and design can be messy, it can also be neat and tidy; it can be on a large scale, covering a whole wall, or in small private notebooks; it can be made while sitting at a computer or sitting on the beach, walking around the class-room, or travelling on a train. Wherever art-making and -learning takes place it should involve some aspect of practical activity. This *making* is the very essence of art and design; without it there would be no opportunity to produce the 'aesthetic significance' (Hickman, 2005) described in Chapter 2.

Children can be observed making things with varying levels of concentration and commit-ment. They will throw themselves into things, play with materials, or try things out. At other times they will be less determined, reluctant or hesitant. There will be times when children want to stop, stand back and look at their work, or other times when they want to put things in a drawer, screw things up or throw things away. This engagement in art-making is similar to that of practising artists as they select, modify, organise, transform, construct, revise and adapt, or reject their ideas, feelings and impulses. For dancers this happens through their bodies in particular spaces, for musicians in noises, rhythms and pulses, and for architects in the buildings, objects or spaces they imagine and build. A role for the teacher, and for other adults, is to help children work in this practical and evolving way, building relationships with their work as it takes shape, helping them respond to the things before them, with increasing thought and reflection, as they build their understanding of visual, spatial and tactile qualities. This increased or developed sense of making, beyond the intuitive or the frustrated, shapes the ways teachers can act and offer intervention, and is indicative of the role of evaluation and review, a characteristic of worthwhile practical learning in art and design activity.

CASE STUDY 3.1
I can't draw dogs
Seated closely side by side, two Year 1 girls begin drawing on recycled paper from the photocopier. It is a wet break and they have access to a limited range of felt pens and pencils. As one girl draws confidently the other copies; beginning with the head of an imaginary flower, she adds petals, a stem and some oversized leaves. In the top corner of the picture a sun appears, with characteristic 'rays'. Seemingly unexpectedly the girl more at ease with drawing begins the outline of a small dog; she appears to do this to a memorised formula, ending at its small upright tail. She adds a collar and a lead, and then a small bowl for water. Meanwhile, frustrated by her own drawing solution for the dog the second girl scribbles over her attempt, stands up and announces that she 'can't draw dogs'.

REFLECTIVE TASK

Read the account described in Case Study 3.1. Imagine you are the class teacher who has observed the announcement of frustration regarding the drawing of dogs. How would you react to this situation? Is it worth reacting to, or would you be tempted to ignore it or suggest that a more positive approach would be useful, perhaps adding that the dog looked fine to you?

One of the challenges for a teacher is knowing how to act in such situations, and knowing what interventions would be useful or appropriate. To help with this process of decision making it is useful to remember what is at stake in terms of learning. In the dog-drawing incident much of the frustration came from the way children compare themselves with others, how they want to be like others, and their developing awareness of other people's drawing solutions. As a result, the interventions made may be focused on supporting the individual's confidence, or suggesting some alternative materials, working in three dimensions with a plastic modelling material, or providing some example pictures of dogs to look at. In all cases, what teachers will try to do is help children make further decisions, to review what they have done in more positive terms, rather than consigning their efforts to the bin. It should be said that this is not always easy, but is made easier by understanding what aspects of learning you are trying to support.

Reflecting on, evaluating and reviewing learning

Where active learning engages children in a process of review and reflection we can describe this learning as *experiential.* Salmon (1998) suggests that in such situations learners are *actively and purposefully engaged in their own learning:*

> In place of top-down knowledge pupils must construct things for themselves. And what is learned must go beyond merely doing things; the learner must learn to reflect on that practical experience, to articulate something of what it means.
>
> (Salmon, 1998, p22)

This reflects the flexibility of experiential learning to respond to personal and cultural needs where '. . . experience is subjective, private, idiosyncratic. For teachers of art and design this is taken for granted. Art is necessarily and deeply personal; both creativity and appreciation are rooted in inner life, individual response, feeling and impulse' (Salmon, 1998, p26). Although many trends in schooling and education appear at odds with these ideas, there have been recent initiatives emphasising the personalised characteristic of experiential learning, as a powerful force in meaningful experiences for pupils at all stages of schooling. For example, the *New Secondary Curriculum Key Stage 3* material builds on principles embedded in the *Every Child Matters* (DfES, 2004) agenda, and aims to promote a more personalised learning experience. The Early Years Foundation Stage (EYFS) reflects a similar commitment, and indications from the *Independent Primary Review* (DCSF, 2009) are that future National Curriculum Key Stages 1 and 2 developments will follow this approach.

> Only the establishment of a sense of trust, on the part of the teacher, may gradually overcome (any) reluctance, and enable children and young children to feel confident in their own personal feeling and reactions.
>
> (Salmon, 1998, p26)

Abbs (1987) describes the process of evaluation and review, central to personal and purposeful learning, as one which 'attempts to organize the complex elements of our aesthetic response' (Abbs, 1987, p61). As children work through their ideas, in a range of materials, they are involved in a series of 'aesthetic responses', and by doing so, they engage in a series of decisions and choices. Children may ask themselves, or be prompted to ask:

> What colour could I add to complement this colour? How could I add some contrast? How can this part be balanced with this? How can a car be made to look

three dimensional? What decorative elements can I add? How can I use pattern to embellish this design? How can this dog be made to look more convincing?

This reflective process results in the objects of art and design, where evaluation informs both the developmental process and the development of the final product. Any final evaluation requires a more distanced *reflection* – one where the maker needs to consider the decisions taken and the choices made. However, you will be aware that when asked children, not unlike adults, find it difficult to express their choice taking and decision making, let alone give an overall view of the thing before them. As such, they need support to develop appropriate vocabulary to articulate their thoughts. As a teacher you should also realise the value of the object itself as evidence of thoughtful making, and a place for further evaluation and reflection. As the cyclical process moves on, 'there is no final stopping place, so criticism and discourse moves on and art, as that awesome activity of creating, begins again' (Abbs, 1987, p62).

The need to be reflective and evaluative during and after art and design activity is encouraged in the later stages of the *EYFS Profile Handbook* (QCA, 2008a), creative development (scale point 9) where children:

> [r]espond to their own work and that of others when exploring and communicating ideas, feelings and preferences through art, music, dance, role play and imaginative play.

It is also reflected in the National Curriculum (DfEE, 1999), which suggests that at Key Stage 1 pupils should be taught to:

1. *review* what they and others have done and *say* what they think and feel about it;
2. identify what they might *change* in their current work or develop in their future work.

And at Key Stage 2 pupils should be taught to:

1. *compare* ideas, methods and approaches in their own and others' work and *say* what they think and feel about them;
2. *adapt* their work according to their views and *describe* how they might develop it further.

In the classroom this process of reviewing, evaluating, changing, comparing, adapting and developing work places demands on pupils to act and think for themselves, and asks teachers to facilitate this kind of working. Salmon (1998) suggests that this facilitation of experiential learning may be difficult to carry out in a climate of schooling, which, at other times, advocates a more teacher-centred model of learning. To develop this important approach to learning you will need to consider approaches you can take, where feedback can develop purposeful art and design responses. Some of these are explored in more detail in *Chapter 8: Assessment, monitoring and feedback.*

REFLECTIVE TASK

Identify something you have learned today. It could be a skill, some knowledge, a key idea or a process of enquiry. Think about that learning and what role reflection and evaluation made to securing your sense of understanding or skill acquisition. Did you find yourself actively reflecting or evaluating during the process of learning? Alternatively, did you find reflection and evaluation more embedded in the whole cycle of learning? What implications does this have for you as a teacher, and how will you provide opportunities to embed reflection and evaluation into teaching and learning?

Describing learning in art and design

What children learn from art and design experiences

As intending teachers you will be aware that the process of planning and preparing lessons asks you to predict what children will learn during that lesson, or series of lessons. This practice is endorsed by Ofsted, carried out in many schools and reflected in some of the planning strategies described in this book (see *Chapter 7: Planning and preparing to teach: ideas into practice*). This is a fairly reasonable process to follow, as it begins to focus your mind towards how you will support any predicted learning. However, for some educators (Eisner, 1985; Hickman, 2000) this level of prediction and anticipation goes against what they feel is good educationally, and what they feel is good about art and design education. They suggest a more open approach to learning and teaching, which encourages flexibility and open-ended responses. They propose that this approach better prepares individuals for the challenges of everyday encounters. There is certainly mileage in this argument and at times it is presented powerfully. At this stage in your development as a teacher we suggest you keep in mind the possibility of working in ways which acknowledge learning through more 'emergent objectives and open approaches', while utilising strategies which make use of more clearly defined and predicted learning.

Eisner (2002) provides more concrete themes to consider as you think about what children learn from art and design experiences, identifying broad areas of learning to which art and design contributes. He suggests that:

> *[w]hat the arts teach, or what students learn when engaged in art activity, using media for artistic expression [is]: learning to* think aesthetically *about images and their creation and helping them advance their ability to* see the world aesthetically *and to describe it in artistically sensitive ways.*
>
> (Eisner, 2002, p75)

This approach of entwining thought with action and perception, and wrapping it in ideas of aesthetic sensitivity may take a little time to grasp, but is worth sticking with as it gives us a good sense of learning in art and design. Eisner (2002) suggests the arts teach us to use our senses and our feelings, sensations and emotions, in the production and appreciation of art and design. Then, he suggests, we take this way of thinking and acting and 'map' it onto the world around us – this way our developed visual, spatial and tactile senses see and notice the things we might otherwise forget. We learn to see iridescent colour in the wings of a magpie, we learn to notice the qualities of light reflected into a room, or the mesmerising shadows from our moving bodies cast across a sunlit pavement. It is these encounters which we can call up when Eisner talks about *artistic* or *aesthetic sensitivity*. Others may offer a different take, but for now it is useful to remember that world, and to describe it in aesthetic terms: of beauty, grace, delicacy, energy, dynamism, or subtlety. In a world where we often forget to sense or see, the arts are a powerful means of restoring a connection with the world, and as such we can encourage children to learn from these powerful encounters.

Eisner continues by suggesting that from art and design experiences pupils will learn to:

1. pay attention to relationships;
2. be flexible in their purposing;
3. use materials as a medium;
4. shape form to create expressive content;
5. exercise their imagination;
6. learn to frame the world from an aesthetic perspective.

(Eisner, 2002, p75)

Eisner's six areas of learning

Paying attention to relationships

In a straightforward way this can be interpreted as remembering to notice things and their details, and then to think about how the detail makes up the whole. These observations can be of things discovered in the made or found world, or in the world of art, craft and design. Children appear to do this sort of thing very spontaneously, and with little hesitation. They notice very small detail in all sorts of things, from coloured stitching to missing buttons. In turn they compose images and objects from lines and marks, from bits and pieces to form organic wholes. On the face of it these compositions seem to be made intuitively, but in an educational context we are striving to develop their visual, spatial and tactile responses, to pay attention to their decisions, their outcomes and their relationships.

Eisner suggests that reaching conclusions about the 'rightness' of the relationships within something produced cannot be reduced to a set of skills or particular knowledge; it also involves feeling. 'A painter, for example, must make choices which depend upon "feel", well before the finishing touch is applied to the work...choices depend on judgement in the absence of rules' (Eisner, 2002, p77).

Being flexible

Flexible purposing involves the ability to shift direction, and change aims, during the course of work; where ends are not set, and means to achieve them constantly revised. To help children work in this way you will need to encourage a relationship with work and ideas which evolves like a conversation, where the teacher and the pupil can respond and adapt, modify and react. This places all sorts of new demands on teachers in terms of planning and accountability, but it adds to the quality of creative art and design work, where ends are not always known or easily predicted.

Eisner is keen for pupils to share experiences which engage them in flexible and open activities. This sort of activity promotes a response from pupils and teachers where ideas and work evolve and change; it involves children and adults learning to improvise. John Dewey (1938) advocated this approach and to some extent Eisner has adapted his ideas, suggesting it refers to the 'improvisational side of intelligence' (Eisner, 2002, p77). Learning to act in this way, Eisner suggests, prepares individuals to respond to the shifting challenges of our lives.

Using materials as a medium

As they exist in the cupboard or the drawer, by the sink or in the stockroom, materials are just that, materials. Boxes of paint, packs of pencils, bags of clay, trays of watercolour, wallets of felt pens, packs of charcoal, tubs of modelling material, reams of paper.

Children pick these things up. They use them to translate and transform their ideas, feelings and impulses into the very objects of art and design. During this process, children use materials to mediate their ideas, and hence materials can be described as media.

To produce an image with intention requires a child to call up, from a repertoire of experience, the skills and knowledge required to get the materials to do what he or she wants, that is they can control the materials as media. This may seem a small point, but it remains an important one, as it suggests that as children learn to use materials to mediate their increasingly sophisticated ideas, they need to be taught appropriate skills, knowledge, and processes.

> *The characteristics of the materials call up different conceptions and skills that function within the limits and possibilities of the material, and it is within the limits and possibilities of the materials that cognition proceeds. As they mature, children's recognition of the material's potential expands, and when their technical skills live up to their expanding conceptions of what they want to create, the quality of their artistry increases.*
>
> (Eisner, 2002, p80)

Figure 3.1 Children's art and design exemplifies some of what they learn; how they pay attention to relationships, remain flexible, and use materials to explore and represent ideas and experiences

Shaping form to create expressive content

When we look at a painting, watch a dance, or move to music, in some way the art form we are engaging with stirs our feelings. When art is really successful some claim it can stir our whole being in an aesthetic way (Abbs, 1996). Artists not only think flexibly and keep their options open, they are skilled in the transformation of materials to mediate their ideas, they remember how all the bits go together to make the whole, and above all they can piece it all together to make it move and stir the souls of others.

For teachers, this remains an area of importance and challenge – how can you help children put all these pieces into place? Indeed very young children might not be aware that the things they make have anything to do with art; after all it is an invented concept, a collection of ideas to articulate something that communities have engaged in for thousands of years. Not only that, the appearance and feel of art changes over time, partly because the very *idea* of art changes. This presents teachers with a problem, in that the thing you will be trying to teach is a slippery idea, and added to this children produce their own *art* apparently oblivious to art outside of school. However, this problem remains the very thing you are trying to teach:

1. to help children develop their own art making activity, beyond the natural or spontaneous;
2. to develop the art and design of children, not in isolation but with reference to the world of art and design;
3. to develop an awareness, understanding and considered appreciation of this world of art and design.

Although some scholars believe that very young children are naturally tuned in to such expressive qualities well before they enter school, there is no evidence to suggest that pre-schoolers can produce such forms on demand or that they know what they are doing when they do so. The development of the imagination, the technical skills and the sensibilities needed to create aesthetic form is much – but not all – of what arts education is about.

(Eisner, 2002, p82)

Being imaginative

One thing art and design education offers is a chance to follow your imagination, to have flights of fancy, or to try out things you may have thought impossible. This almost goes without saying, and in schools we see young children engaged in this active imagining with little reservation, making reference to prior experience and memory.

Eisner suggests that the benefit of such 'whimsy' is not only self satisfying, but that the distorting of reality makes reality even more real; it draws our attention to things: 'the imaginative image...functions as a template by which we can reorganise our perceptions of the world' (Eisner, 2002, p83).

As you read stories to children you will notice how, increasingly, they make distinctions between the imagined and the real. They will produce drawings or make models which allow them to test out this understanding further, playing with imaginative ideas which encourage looking at reality with fresh eyes. Good art does the same thing – it is a bit like refreshing a computer screen; you are encouraged by good imaginative art to look at the world with refreshed vision.

Learning to see the world from an aesthetic perspective

The *wide-awakeness* (Greene, 1995, in Eisner, 2002, p83) described above helps us to see the world from a new perspective, through a new lens. The *wide-awakeness* (Eisner, 2002, p83 explores the ideas of Greene, 1995) described above helps us to see the world from a new perspective, through a new lens.

Seeing the rock aesthetically, or hearing a wonderful piece of music or experiencing a fine play is more than becoming aware of its qualities. It is a way of being moved, of finding out something about our capacity to be moved... In its best moments it is a way of experiencing joy.

(Eisner, 2002, p84)

You are challenged with the role of helping children towards 'experiencing the fullness of our emotional life...about becoming alive' (Eisner, 2002, p85). This will not always be easy or straightforward, but will be rewarding when it happens. It may occur during a modelling activity, where you witness children using clay to examine experiences and imagination, where they become immersed in the fantasy of their making, where groups and individuals are moved beyond the mundane, the ordinary, and the everyday. It may be hard to pin down with objectives, as it may be beyond what you predicted, but it will be valuable.

Describing learning in these ways does not readily, or immediately, translate to lesson objectives or descriptions of learning intentions. However, you will see in the detail that follows how more specific learning contributes to the six areas described above.

Learning in and through art and design

The subject of art and design, like other subjects, has its own knowledge base, its own skills and processes. As such, progressive and developmental *learning in* art and design is described in these areas of knowledge, skills and processes. This is reflected in the National Curriculum (DfEE, 1999) which describes a subject or discipline based approach.

You will also encounter situations where learning is described as being *through* art and design. In this description learning does not reside in the knowledge, skills or processes of the subject, but beyond the subject, and usually in the children engaged in an activity. Learning is extrinsic to the subject, it is a more child-centred orientation, in that the development of wellbeing, temperament or creative capacities in individuals are offered as signs of learning.

Dick Field (1973) commented on the significant change and difference between the two approaches:

> It can be argued that, in reaction to the concept of 'education through art', the development of the concept of 'education in art' became inevitable. If the one focuses attention on the pupil, the latter calls attention to the discipline of art; if the former involves minimal teaching, the latter proclaims there is material that needs teaching; if for the former the practice of art is sufficient, the latter calls attention to the claims of aesthetics, criticism and art history.
>
> (Field, 1973, p156)

These two areas of learning are very useful in shaping balanced learning outcomes, and planning and preparing to teach.

Learning through art and design

An education *through* art sees art in schools as serving purposes other than art and design – these may be cultural, social, economic and psychological and are often centred on the pupil. The activities are often described as emphasising the processes of activity and creative making rather than the art and design products or artefacts. The processes are seen as significant to individuals, their wellbeing and their social interactions. Learning might include the following.

- Therapy: 'Art is used as a vehicle for self-expression. It is seen as something contributing to mental health'.
- Creative thinking: 'Art, it is claimed, has an especially important contribution to make to the development of creative thinking'.
- Cross-curricular contributions: 'Art is seen as a handmaiden to concept formation'.
- Physiological development: 'Art is said to develop fine muscles hence improve the child's co-ordination'.

(Eisner, 1972, p8)

Working on a large-scale class project, children may learn to share and co-operate, to value other ideas, to listen and compromise. The project may enhance learning in history or develop spatial awareness explored in mathematics. Working on individual pieces following periods of standardised tests in other subjects, art and design may offer a release, a chance to relax or let off steam.

In all these cases the learning experience, albeit valuable, does not draw on the intrinsic qualities of art and design. Instead the learning described above, whether personal, emotional, or social, could be gained from any number of subjects. Hence we would say things have been learned *through art and design.*

The National Society for Education in Art and Design (NSEAD) (2009) suggest that learning through art and design for the twenty-first century involves allowing children to develop their own thinking and questioning skills. This will enable children to gain knowledge and understanding of the world around them and its people, and prepare them for the future by:

- introducing a unique visual language;
- combining ideas and thoughts with senses and emotions;
- valuing diversity and individuality;
- encouraging intellectual and physical development;
- allowing time for reflection;
- promoting innovation, risk taking and problem solving;
- developing a positive awareness of different cultures and traditions;
- allowing children to articulate their own ideas and develop the ability to make critical judgements;
- promoting playfulness and curiosity;
- developing sensitivity, empathy and intuitiveness;
- encouraging self-awareness and awareness of others;
- enhancing the ability to collaborate with other people and take the views of other people into account;
- building independence;
- increasing their tolerance for ambiguity;
- making links between unusual concepts and circumstances;
- developing confidence;
- promoting the acquisition of new skills;
- developing the imagination;
- encouraging experimental approaches;
- being excited, absorbed, and motivated.

Learning in art and design

An education *in* art is concerned with the subject of art, its history, its tradition, its processes, knowledge and skills, objects and artefacts. Learning is concerned with the things that are unique and intrinsic to art and design:

The following areas of learning in art and design reflect the requirements of the National Curriculum (DfEE, 1999) and are adapted from the National Curriculum Council's publication (NCC) *The arts 5–16: Practice and innovation* (1990: 11–15).

We shall explore each of these areas in detail in the following sections.

Processes:
Explore
Develop
Investigate
Make
Present
Review
Evaluate

Skills:
Perception
Production
Discussion

Knowledge/Understanding:
Aesthetic: Visual – line, tone, pattern, colour, texture, form, space, shape. Composition – balance, harmony, contrast, repetition, symmetry
Art Experiences: painting, drawing, printmaking, collage, montage, textiles, construction, modelling, lens-based media and ICT.
Contextual: artists, craftspeople, designers, architects, periods, genres, styles.

adapted from: National Curriclum (DfEE, 1999) and the National Curriculum Council's (NCC) publication
The arts 5–16: practice and innovation (1990, pp11–15)

Figure 3.2 Areas of learning in art and design

PRACTICAL TASK PRACTICAL TASK **PRACTICAL TASK** PRACTICAL TASK **PRACTICAL TASK**Practical Task

On a sheet of paper, record all the things children learn from art and design experiences. Organise and group the learning under two headings: 'learning *through* art and design' and 'learning *in* art and design'. Compare the two lists and consider how the two areas of learning support each other. For example, developing skills and knowledge about paint and colour provides a springboard for children to be able to explore colour and paint in more imaginative ways, thus developing their creative capacities.

Processes

Exploring and developing

Exploratory work lies at the heart of art and design activity. It encourages children to work from memory, imagination and first hand experience to explore a range of ideas and starting points. This approach allows an opening up of these ideas and interests, culminating in finished objects or remaining tentative or exploratory. By exploring materials and ideas, visual, spatial and tactile qualities, children are encouraged to see how things might work out, to test out what might be possible, to see the limitations or potential of different combinations. The teacher has an important role to play in the development of these explorations. By prompting, questioning, challenging and supporting, the teacher provides an environment and the time for things to evolve, for experiences to take shape (NCC, 1990, p11).

Investigating

The process of investigation can be applied to the materials associated with art and design, and to the visual, tactile and spatial qualities of art and design. Equally the process of investigation can be extended as a tool for investigating a particular context, a process of investigative enquiry. This provides opportunities for children to look at and notice things, by investigating the interactions of visual, spatial and tactile qualities. These can be recorded with cameras, with drawings, with rubbings, with impressions made in clay or with collections of objects.

Making

'Making involves the forming of objects or events, which embody and represent artists' conceptions, intentions and perceptions' (NCC, 1990, p11). These are not 'simply translated into visual form', they may begin as vague nuances; some notes, a sketch, a phrase. Ideas and beginnings are then 'reassessed, reworked, refined' and reshaped. Children and teachers establish a conversation with the evolving work, offering feedback, support and challenge, as children gain experience in translating and transforming their initial investigations and explorations into work that reflects their intentions (NCC, 1990, p11).

Presenting

Although presenting does not feature as a process in the National Curriculum (1999), the National Curriculum Council (NCC, 1990, p12) identified presenting as a relevant process for arts education. During exploration, investigation and making it is particularly useful to share ideas. This can be a sharing of initial ideas, responses to starting points, personal responses to themes and evolving imagery and objects. The audience at this stage may be intimate and known, perhaps a group of peers and the teacher. Not all this early development work is intended for more public display. However, some work will be made more public, and as such forms of presentation are worth early consideration. This will place some boundaries on how work can be developed. It might be that it is for a display and needs to be a certain size, the imagery may become web-based and will need to be scanned, the completed objects may sit on a shelf or in a display cabinet, hang from the ceiling or be flicked through in a book (NCC, 1990, p12).

Evaluating

Children are asked to make increasingly refined judgements about their work and the work of others. This demands not only skills of discussion, but observation and perception, as well as knowledge and understanding. Perhaps the key contributor to observing and evaluating work is increased and developed language, and art-based vocabulary. As children move towards Key Stage 2 they may feel more comfortable in expressing ideas about balance, tone, strength or subtlety in work.

Responding

'The arts have to be experienced first hand wherever possible' (NCC, 1990, p12). Arts education has a 'responsibility to extend young people's sensibilities to the arts and the range and depth of their art experience and understanding' (NCC, 1990, p12). In art and design the range of artists extends to craftspeople and designers working in different times and cultures. The range should include different styles, genres and traditions, in galleries or museums, or working with artists in schools, or in reproduction form.

Skills

Development and maturation in the arts is dependent upon skills and expertise which need to be learnt and practised.

Perceptual skills

'Observations are central to many art forms' (NCC, 1990, p14). In visual art they are closely linked to the tradition of developing skills of observational drawing: for its own sake, to increase awareness of the environment, as a basis for representations, descriptions or accounts of actual experience. Perceptual skills are also used to 'shape and organise materials into appropriate forms'. They are also used in the process of discriminating and reflecting on the work of others, and recognising the ways in which 'artists acknowledge and use audience/spectator perceptions' (NCC, 1990, p14).

Productive skills

'Making involves skill and control in the manipulation of chosen media' (NCC, 1990, p14). However, learning skills that remain out of context or without significance will be 'frustrating and self-defeating'. Similarly, belief in creativity and spontaneity at the expense of skill learning can result in poorly expressed ideas and frustration. 'Teaching skills in appropriate media and for a purpose is an essential part of creative work' (NCC, 1990, p14).

Discussion skills

Pupils need to be encouraged to consider the role and importance of dialogue in developing work and ideas about work. A developing vocabulary is required to make judgements about their own work and that of others; talking to each other, making notes, talking about artists' work, looking and talking in galleries, listening to artists and gallery educators.

Knowledge and understanding

To support the development of the processes and skills described above, the National Curriculum (1999) and NCC (1990) suggest that children are taught knowledge and understanding in the following areas.

1. *Knowledge of aesthetic, visual, spatial and tactile elements.*

   Sometimes referred to as 'qualities', the elements are described as colour, pattern, texture or surface, line, tone, shape, form and space. When explored through different materials and combined, these elements have the potential to serve a range of intentions. In turn, the act of combining hints at a further area of visual knowledge: composition. As children's pictorial enquiry develops and their image making is refined, composition plays an important role in its organisation and resolution. Compositional qualities of balance, harmony, tension, space, illusion, tone, intensity or energy can be explored.

2. *Knowledge of materials and art experiences.*

   Art experiences (also referred to as processes in the National Curriculum) include: painting, drawing, printmaking, collage, montage, textiles, construction, modelling, lens-based media and ICT.

3. *Knowledge of artists, designers and craftspeople working in different times and cultures.*

   This important area of knowledge includes an introduction to examples of art, craft and design from different periods or genres.

Further detail of these areas of learning can be found in *Chapter 4: Knowledge and understanding: progression of experiences and processes*.

Values and attitudes

'Attitudes that should be encouraged' include:

- confidence;
- willingness;
- readiness;
- openness;
- curiosity;
- sensitivity;
- sense of self-worth;
- commitment;
- care;
- attention.

(NCC, 1990, p15)

REFLECTIVE TASK

This chapter has explored a number of ideas, from broader general themes in arts learning, to more detailed examples of learning in art and design. Making a step towards thinking about art and design in these ways is a positive one, it helps you move nearer to thinking about the activities you teach, and the way you will be able to describe them educationally. The example in Figure 3.3 provides an account of learning in a cross-curricular project based on the local environment. Read the account and use the detail round the edge to describe learning, both in art and design and through art and design. In addition you will be able to speculate when children are engaging with the six characteristics of learning in the arts described by Eisner (2002).

Consider your development needs with reference to the *continuum of experience, needs, confidence and support* detailed in the Introduction and developed in *Chapter 5: Considering teachers and teaching: principles*. What is your understanding of active and experiential learning, Eisner's (2002) six areas of learning, or learning in and through art and design? Identify areas of learning where you need to develop your subject knowledge. Your awareness can be supported by talking to teachers and children, observing teachers and children, reading books, visiting websites, talking to peers.

Chapter 4: Knowledge and understanding: progression of experiences and processes develops some of the areas of learning described in this chapter, with more detail. In particular it connects learning to practical activities and establishes these in sequences of progression.

A SUMMARY OF KEY POINTS

> **Art and design involves practical and active experiences.**

> **Experiences are developed through a process of engagement, reflection and evaluation.**

> **Learning takes place during experiences; it is evident in the processes of experience.**

> **Learning can be described in terms of processes, knowledge, skills, and values.**

> **Other people support and contribute to learning experiences.**

Learning in art and design

Processes
- explore
- develop
- investigate
- make
- evaluate

Knowledge
- visual qualities
- materials
- artists, craftspeople and designers

Skills
- production
- perception
- discussion

Values
- confidence
- willingness
- openness
- sensitivity
- commitment
- care
- attention

Learning through art and design
- creative development
- cross-curricular development
- personal development

The 'Overlooked'

The line of children looked relatively conventional as they walked purposefully down the local high street. At specific points on their journey the class broke into small groups, supervised by parent helpers, the class teacher and two Year 3 teaching students. Each group of children had been given a set of specific instructions to follow, with the aim of supporting their local environment project by gathering visual information:

1. Take a photograph looking down, looking up and looking straight ahead.
2. Produce a line drawing of a pattern occurring in the made environment.
3. Make a rubbing of some texture.
4. Collect 4 examples of environmental text.
5. Record 4 words reflecting the mood of your stopping point.
6. Draw a doorway or entrance you can see.

Each group was reminded to *'keep looking and to notice things we would otherwise not see, remembering to look high and low'*. 'Miss, did you see that notice? It said someone had died there during the plague... We did about that last year, with Mr Robins.'

In the low-key shopping centre the children sat down in their small groups, beside long pieces of unrolled white paper. 'Remember, your group is drawing a panorama of all the things at ground level, your group is drawing things at head height and your group are looking right up there... Only use the marker pens to produce line drawings and, if you find them useful, use one of the viewfinders to find interesting bits...We'll be putting these drawings together as one big drawing back in the classroom...We've got about 25 minutes...'

The following day the class began sorting their visual information, recounting what they had seen, sharing their observations and asking questions: 'Those legs look like a dog's legs... They are... Look, that group's done his head... He was a guide dog in the shopping centre.'

The teacher shared some of her observations of the group and suggested the material collected could be used to make a large class montage depicting the variety and interest in their local environment.

What children learn from experiences:

1. to pay attention to relationships;
2. to be flexible in their purposing;
3. to use materials as a medium;
4. to shape form to create expressive content;
5. to exercise their imagination;
6. to learn to frame the world from an aesthetic perspective (Eisner, 2002).

Figure 3.3 An example of learning outside the classroom

MOVING *ON* > > > > > > MOVING *ON* > > > > > > MOVING *ON*

Continue to extend and develop your understanding of active and experiential learning, by observing children, by reading, and by talking to others about the processes involved in learning.

REFERENCES REFERENCES **REFERENCES** REFERENCES **REFERENCES** REFERENCES

Abbs, P (1987) (ed) *Living powers: The arts in education*. Lewes: Falmer.

Abbs, P (1996) Making the art beat faster, in Dawtrey, L, Jackson, T, Masterton, M, and Meecham, P (eds) *Critical studies and modern art.* London: Yale University Press.

DCSF (2009) *Independent Primary Review*. DCSF. Available to download at www.publications.teachernet.gov.uk

Dewey, J (1938) Experience and Education. New York: Macmillan.

DfEE (1999) *The National Curriculum*. London: HMSO.

DfES (2004) *Every Child Matters: Change for children*. Nottingham: DfES Publications.

Eisner, EW (1972) *Educating artistic vision*. London: Macmillan.

Eisner, EW (1985) *The educational imagination*: *On the design and evaluation of school programs*. London: Macmillan.

Eisner, EW (2002) *The arts and the creation of mind*. Yale: Yale University Press.

Field, D (1973) Art and art education, in Field, D and Newick, J *The study of education and art*. London: Routledge and Kegan Paul.

Hickman, R (2000) (ed) *Art education 11–18: Meaning, purpose and direction.* London: Continuum.

Hickman, R (2005) *Why we make art and why it is taught*. Bristol: Intellect Books.

National Curriculum Council (NCC) Arts in Schools Project Team (1990) *The arts 5–16: Practice and innovation.* Harlow: Oliver and Boyd.

Prentice, R (1998) (ed) *Teaching art and design: Addressing issues and identifying directions*. London: Cassell.

Prentice, R (1999) Art: Visual thinking, in Riley, J and Prentice, R (eds) *The curriculum for 7–11 year olds.* London: Paul Chapman Publishing.

Prentice, R (2003) Changing places, in Addison, N and Burgess, L. (eds) *Issues in art and design teaching*. London: RoutledgeFalmer.

QCA (2008) *Early Years Foundation Stage Profile Handbook*. London: HMSO.

Salmon, P (1998) Experiential Learning in Prentice, R (ed) *Teaching Art and Design*. London: Cassell.

www.nsead.org.uk

http://www.nsead.org/primary/national/rationale.aspx accessed July 2009.

4
Knowledge and understanding: progression of experiences and processes

Chapter objectives

By the end of this chapter you will have:

- **developed an awareness of knowledge and understanding appropriate for primary art and design;**
- **considered visual, tactile and spatial elements as valuable aspects of art and design learning;**
- **developed an understanding of progression across experiences, processes and materials;**
- **developed an understanding of the potential of artists, craftspeople and designers to support and develop learning in art and design;**
- **developed your awareness of appropriate vocabulary to support knowledge and understanding in art and design.**

This chapter addresses the following Standards for QTS: **Q14**, **Q15**, **Q27**.

Key themes: visual, tactile and spatial elements; experiences; processes; materials; progression; development; vocabulary; resources; ICT and digital media; artists; genres; styles; traditions.

Introduction

Chapter 1: Art and design in the primary school: the current scene, and *Chapter 3: Considering learners and learning: principles and practice*, introduced the national requirements and expectations for primary art and design. These are established in the Early Years Foundation Stage (DCSF, 2008), creative development strand, developed through the National Curriculum (DfEE, 1999) art and design programme of study, and extended in the National Curriculum (DfEE, 1999) art and design breadth of study.

This chapter will support your awareness of learning in art and design within these contexts, with a particular focus on knowledge and understanding. These areas of learning, while not expressed as explicitly in the Early Years Foundation Stage (DCSF, 2008) profile, build on creative development expectations. These encourage the development of visual, tactile and spatial awareness and understanding, as well as the use and control of materials. Children should have opportunity to:

- capture experiences, using a variety of different media;
- respond in a variety of ways to what they see, hear, smell, touch and feel;
- express and communicate their ideas, thoughts and feelings by using a widening range of materials, suitable tools, imaginative and role play, movement, designing and making, and a variety of songs and musical instruments;
- explore colour, texture, shape, form and space in two and three dimensions (EYFS Statutory Framework, DCSF, 2008, p48).

Progression indicated in the National Curriculum across Key Stages 1 and 2

During Key Stage 1 pupils develop their creativity and imagination by exploring the visual, tactile and sensory qualities of materials and processes. They learn about the role of art, craft and design in their environment. They begin to understand colour, shape, space, pattern and texture and use them to represent their ideas and feelings.

During Key Stage 2 pupils develop their creativity and imagination through more *complex* activities. These help to *build on their skills* and *improve their control* of materials, tools and techniques. They *increase their critical awareness* of the roles and purposes of art, craft and design in different times and cultures. They become *more confident* in using visual and tactile elements and materials and processes to communicate what they see, feel and think.

Across both key stages teaching should ensure that *investigating and making* includes *exploring and developing ideas* and *evaluating and developing work.*

These processes should be supported by **knowledge and understanding of**:

1. **the visual and tactile elements**: colour, pattern, texture, line, tone, shape, form and space, and how these can be combined and organised for different purposes;
2. **materials and processes**: drawing, painting, printmaking, collage, digital media, textiles, and sculpture, and how these can be matched to ideas and intentions;
3. **artists, craftspeople and designers** working in different times and cultures, in a variety of genres, styles and traditions (DfEE, 1999, p118).

To support and develop your understanding, this chapter will consider each area of knowledge and understanding in turn. It is worth noting that while the areas appear distinct, in practice these areas of knowledge and understanding are interconnected and inter-related. Exploring colour will inevitably involve a range of appropriate materials, and will necessitate understanding of artistic processes, probably through some form of painting activity. In turn the work of artists, craftspeople and designers can be integrated into the process of learning to support and develop work. A challenge you will face as a teacher involves making connections between these areas, for example linking appropriate drawing materials with aspects of work exploring tone, and supporting with useful examples from artistic practices. As a result learning experiences will feel contextualised and more robust.

Knowledge and understanding of visual and tactile elements

Although the National Curriculum (DfEE, 1999) describes the elements of colour, pattern, texture, line, tone, shape, form and space, as visual and tactile, elsewhere we have extended this phrase to *visual, tactile and spatial*.

Bowden (2006) suggests that when considering the visual, tactile and spatial elements in primary art and design it is useful to:

- **start with an observed or experienced source**: 'a way of introducing primary pupils to the visual elements is to develop their understanding by using first-hand observational (*or other sensory*) source, rather than starting with the total abstraction of "basic design" (*visual, tactile or spatial*) activities' (Bowden, 2006, p36).

This may involve children in the close examination of texture or surface qualities of found objects using viewfinders, or noting the tonal range of a landscape scene with squares of tonal papers, identifying a colour scheme in an artist's work or feeling the form of branches and stems.

- *link the visual elements with media*: 'each of the visual elements has associations with a particular medium...between drawing and line and tone, painting and colour, printmaking with the exploration of surface and texture, clay and three-dimensional materials with space and form' (Bowden, 2006, p37). It will come as little surprise that these associations are often blurred, for example where artists employ colour in sculpture or explore texture with paint. However, you will find it beneficial during the planning and preparation stages to make close links between materials and visual elements. This will help your focus when teaching, and support feedback opportunities to help children develop their visual, spatial and tactile awareness and understanding.

- *knowledge of the visual elements*: 'Some aspects of learning related to the visual elements involve specific and measurable knowledge, and can thus be taught specifically and progressively' (Bowden, 2006, p37). However, Bowden adds that in addition 'pupils need to be given the opportunity to experiment with media to discover for themselves the "rules"' (Bowden, 2006, p37).

This interplay between experimentation and observation of rules is symptomatic of art and design activity. Artists move between the conventional and the original as they seek ways which excite or intrigue. As an intending teacher you will be able to work with activities focused on transferring knowledge or understanding, from practical demonstration or inter-active whiteboard exemplification, to activities inviting awareness through discovery. A characteristic of good teaching in such a context is supporting children's visual, tactile and spatial development, through challenging activity. This approach encourages consid-ered and controlled decisions and actions, but avoids over prescription. For example, children can be asked to 'look closely at a natural form and...use appropriate media to compare thick lines with thin, hard with soft, furry with crisp' (Bowden, 2006, p37).

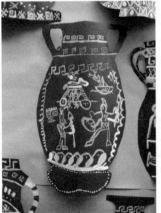

Figure 4.1 Children explore and skilfully control materials and processes, demonstrating their understanding of visual, tactile and spatial qualities, in a range of contexts

PRACTICAL TASK PRACTICAL TASK **PRACTICAL TASK** PRACTICAL TASK **PRACTICAL TASK**

An approach to supporting and developing children's knowledge and understanding in art and design is through 'challenge'. Providing children with particular challenges establishes a boundary within which children can explore materials, processes and visual, tactile and spatial elements, while avoiding overtly teacher-led experiences and outcomes.

Read the list below and keep it in mind as you explore the chapter.

Challenge pupils to:

- mix a range of 10 green hues, using cyan blue, Prussian blue, and yellow;
- apply the same colour to the paper using five different brush strokes;
- layer a lighter colour over a darker colour with an opaque paint;
- combine two materials to show contrasting textures, ribbed, granulated, and coarse;
- remove graphite pencil with an eraser to show highlights and reflections;
- use continuous lines to show movement in physical education dance routines;
- identify a plant motif, cut it out of paper, repeat and rotate it to produce a sequence;
- organise repeated construction units to build a symmetrical image;
- sort and sequence tonal papers from light to dark;
- combine tonal papers to show contrast.

Refer to visual, tactile and spatial elements below and extend the list of control challenges to include shape, form and space.

Colour

Lots of primary art and design activities involve children exploring colour with interest and excitement. Paint is clearly a favourite and appropriate material with which to explore properties of colour; the range of coloured materials indicated below will all provide children with opportunities to develop their knowledge and understanding of colour. Children will use colour to decorate and embellish drawings and models, they will use colour to express ideas, feelings and impulses. Increasingly children will learn qualities of colours and coloured materials, combining colours and materials to show contrast, vibrancy or subtlety.

Key terms
- Primary colour: colour that cannot be obtained by mixing.
- Secondary colour: made from mixtures of two primaries.
- Tertiary colour: a mix of one primary and one secondary, effectively three colours.
- Complementary colours: colours which react most with each other and are opposite on the colour wheel.
- Discords: secondary-to-secondary pairings of colours.
- Tone: lightness and darkness of colour.
- Hue: the property of a colour that enables it to be identified as red, yellow etc.
- Intensity: saturation, the brightness or brilliance of a colour.
- Intensity: chroma, the purity of a colour.
- Monochrome: single colour scheme.
- Achromatic: black and white.

Qualities of colour vocabulary: cold, warm, bold, hot, temperate, natural, industrial, saturated, bright, intense, subtle, deep, delicate, strong, fierce, quiet, loud, limited-range, broad-range, contrast, harmony, block-colour, colour-field, opaque, transparent, translucent, iridescent, fluorescent, tint, shade, complementary, discordant, symbolic, vibrant, energetic, tranquil.

Application of colour vocabulary: over-lay, under-paint, thick, impasto, thin, wash, scratch, dry-brush, stipple, scrub.

Materials for colour: powder paint, ready-mixed paint, colour pencils, felt pens, water soluble pencils, oil pastels, chalk pastels, pens, inks, fabric dyes, fabric paints, coloured papers.

Observed or experienced source: plastic toys, wooden toys, fruit and vegetables, wools, threads and fabrics, plastic bottle tops, food packaging, flower heads, leaves, reflections in water, market stalls, supermarket aisles, factory production lines, car parks, books on shelves, coats on pegs.

Examples of art movements: Fauvism, Expressionism, De Stijl.

Examples of artists, craftspeople or designers: André Derain, Henri Matisse, Franz Marc, Piet Mondrian, Niki de St Phalle, Fiona Rae, Howard Hodgkin, Jim Lambie, Ian Davenport, Peter Doig.

Pattern

Pattern making provides opportunities for children to explore shapes and spaces to generate repeated and sequenced patterns, forming patterns with found and made objects and a wide range of graphic media. For some children, generating pattern is an important feature of their drawing and image making repertoire and they happily and willingly create patterns from a range of objects or materials. Pattern making provides opportunities to develop cross-curricular understanding and awareness, with close links to mathematics. Traditional methods of printmaking offer opportunities to explore repeated imagery and are appropriate art and design experiences allied to pattern. Children will draw repeated and sequenced shapes, use stencils to create geometric shapes, colour sequences on squared paper, organise sequenced beads on threads, and play with symmetry by folding paper.

Vocabulary: shape, space, motif, sequence, design, repeat, rotate, mirror, order, organise, predict, grid, divide, surface, embellish, decorate, mosaic, tessellate, surface, rhythm.

Materials for pattern making: torn and cut contrasting paper, geometric grid paper, pens, pencils and graphic media, relief printing surfaces (found and made objects, polystyrene sheet), repeated units (construction materials, stickers, sequins, transfer letters, stencilled letters).

Observed or experienced source: architectural features, columns, arches, mullions, leaded windows, brick work, manhole covers, leaf shapes, fabric patterns, flower heads, petals, wallpapers, fencing, ironwork, road markings, floor coverings.

Examples of art movements: Cubism, Vorticism.

Examples of artists, craftspeople or designers: Georges Braque, Pablo Picasso, Wyndham Lewis, Peter Randall Page, Frank Stella, Sonia Delaunay, Sol LeWitt, Friedensreich Hundertwasser.

Texture

Texture refers to the surface appearance of objects both found and made. The appearance of the surface can either be determined by touch or sight. Working in the classroom, along corridors, in the school grounds and beyond the school gates, texture and surfaces invite children to explore through their senses of sight and touch. Texture is a visual and tactile element rich in opportunity; it challenges children to recreate complex surface qualities, sometimes initiated with rubbings and extended by combining materials. Children will use wax crayons to make rubbings, tear up paper and card, mix sand into paint, run pebbles and sand through their hands, stroke animals and layer materials.

Vocabulary: smooth, rough, delicate, uneven, impasto, crumbly, ribbed, dull, shiny, reflective, coarse, granulated, glossy, matte, layer, uncover, reveal, surface, embed, relief, undulating, contour.

Materials for exploring texture: torn and cut paper, range of pencils HB to 6B, eraser, charcoal, chalk, oil pastels, glue, sand, wax crayons.

Observed or experienced source: gravel, sand, glass, concrete, wood, bark, leaves, pebbles, acorns, plastic toys, cutlery, grass, seeds, fruit and vegetable surfaces and flesh, plastic household electrical items (telephone, calculator, PC keyboard).

Examples of art movements: Expressionism, Abstract Expressionism.

Examples of artists, craftspeople or designers: Constantin Brancusi, Jackson Pollock, Jasper Johns, Gillian Ayres, Chris Ofili, Trisha Lamoreaux, Antoni Tapiez, Cy Twombly, Alice Kettle.

Line

The building blocks of drawing, lines come in all shapes and sizes; they combine to form shapes, patterns, tones and textures. Lines can be interpreted in the environment, in found and made objects. They appear where one shape or object or surface or colour meets another, and gives the appearance of a 'line'. In addition they are added to environments to mark out and delineate spaces, from football pitches to parking bays. Children will use line to show outlines of animals, make shapes for figures, show movement in drawings, and to show movement of firework explosions.

Vocabulary: straight, curved, fine, thick, horizon, outline, wavy, zigzag, organic, rhythmic, industrial, delicate, heavy, dash, dot, spot, splodge, mark, point perspective, proportion, vanishing point, gesture, cross-hatching, direction, enclosure, edge, movement, direction, rhythm.

Materials for exploring line: pencils, colour pencils, felt pens, water soluble pencils, oil pastels, chalk pastels, pens, fine line pens, marker pens, threads, string, rope, torn and cut paper, masking tape, plastic insulating tape.

Observed or experienced source: train lines, street lamps, road markings, window frames, star constellations, cut fruit, leaf veins, bark, wire fencing, branches, mechanical objects, pens and pencils in storage containers, books on shelves.

Examples of art movements: Constructivism, Futurism, Abstract Expressionism.

Examples of artists, craftspeople and designers: Liubov Popova, Giacomo Balla, Jackson Pollock, Patrick Caulfield, Michael Craig-Martin, Sol LeWitt, David Hockney, Julian Opie.

Tone

Tone is the appearance of reflected or absorbed light on or from surfaces and objects. Children will enjoy opportunities to examine extremes of tone with directional light, and the use of tone to create the illusion of form on a two-dimensional surface. Examining tonal ranges in coloured surfaces will engage and challenge children, demanding that they look and notice colour qualities more carefully. Children will mix light and dark tones of single colours, compare 'light' and 'dark' colours, paint night-time scenes, enjoy lighting rooms with torches, show contrast in firework paintings, and play with silhouettes.

Vocabulary: light, dark, gradient, shade, dramatic, contrast, depth, reflection, highlight, shadow, boundary, scale, grey scale, monochrome, accent.

Materials for exploring tone: range of pencils HB to 6B, eraser, charcoal, black and white paint, range of tonal papers, black ink, fine line pens, marker pens, chalk, conté crayon, black and white wax crayons, complementary paint colours (used to mix 'grey' tones).

Observed or experienced source: fruit, vegetables, toys, mechanical objects, faces, fabrics and clothes, lit with directional light, townscapes and architecture, archways, doorways, containers holding objects.

Examples of artists, craftspeople or designers: Rembrandt, John Constable, Pablo Picasso, Peter Randall Page, Vincent van Gogh, Vija Celmins, Chuck Close, Paul Morrison, Clare Woods.

Shape

Children explore shape as part of their everyday experiences. They gain an understanding of two- and three-dimensional shapes, through touch, sight and exploration. Exploring shape provides an opportunity for children to develop their awareness of the 'boundaries' common to two-dimensional shapes and the space occupied by three-dimensional shapes. Art and design activities concerned with shape encourage children to make use of materials to articulate shape and create the illusion of three-dimensional shapes. Children will cut and paste shapes from paper, combine shapes to make houses and people and cars, use shapes to decorate and make patterns, and make shapes of animals with half-eaten toast.

Vocabulary: organic, mechanical, regular, irregular, concentric, repeated, rotated, tessellated, angular, flowing, solid, movement, rhythmic.

Materials for exploring shape: torn and cut paper and card, pre-cut repeated paper shapes, pencils, colour pencils, felt pens, water soluble pencils, oil pastels, chalk pastels, pens, fine line pens, marker pens, repeated objects (construction units, buttons, sequins).

Observed or experienced source: archways, doorways, windows, pathways, fields, fruit and vegetables, mechanical objects, toys, coats on pegs, leaves, fabric prints, cars, lorry and tractor outlines, animal outlines, maps.

Examples of art movements: Orphism, Cubism, Suprematism, Optical art.

Examples of artists, craftspeople and designers: Robert Delaunay, Kasimir Malevich, Victor Vasarely, Henri Matisse, Bridget Riley, Paul Morrison.

Form

Children explore form by picking up, handling, and clutching three-dimensional objects. They learn through touch about contour, mass, weight and balance. Children will play with clay, pushing and pulling it to form shapes which roll, stand up, balance, or join together, stretch across gaps or fill small spaces. They will balance objects on other objects, pick up pebbles and build towers, and construct spaceships from scrap materials.

Vocabulary: organic, geometric, regular, irregular, weight, force, balance, structure, space.

Materials for exploring form: plastic modelling material (playdough, salt dough, plastic modelling clay, clay, air-drying clay), mod-roc, paper pulp, construction materials (card, paper, tape, staples, glue guns, art straws), manufactured plastic and wooden construction materials, wire, cane and willow, scrap materials.

Observed or experienced source: trees, branches, cars, fish, mammals, insects, reptiles, monuments, buildings and towers, bridges, domestic appliances, human figures.

Examples of art movements: site specific, land art, environmental, abstract.

Examples of artists, craftspeople and designers: Jean Tinguely, Andy Goldsworthy, Naum Gabo, Dale Chihuly, Anish Kapoor, Louise Bourgeois, Rachel Whiteread, Antony Gormley, Barry Flanagan, Peter Randall Page.

Space

Space exists around, between, or adjacent to, shapes and form. Children explore 'spaces' in many different ways. They learn relationships between spaces, and sizes of spaces, by filling containers with sand and water, by threading arms through small gaps and poking sticks between railings or putting stones inside shoes. They will force toys into full boxes, stuff drawers with clothes, and pack and re-pack suitcases and rucksacks. In drawings children will begin to organise events, objects and people across a drawing space, making use of scale and overlap.

Vocabulary: boundary, edge, overlap, negative, positive, gap, hole, aperture, ground, balance, relation, size.

Materials for exploring space: plastic modelling material (playdough, salt dough, plastic modelling clay, clay, air-drying clay), mod roc, paper pulp, construction materials (card, paper, tape, staples, glue guns, art straws), manufactured plastic and wooden construction materials, wire, cane and willow, scrap materials.

Observed or experienced source: boxes and containers, fencing, openings in buildings, courtyards, cupboards, maps.

Examples of art movements: site specific, land art, environmental, abstract.

Examples of artists, craftspeople and designers: Richard Long, Antonio Gaudí, Alexander Calder, Henry Moore, David Smith, Barry Flanagan, Antony Gormley.

CASE STUDY 4.1
The deep blue sea
A mixed EYFS and Year 1 group are currently exploring Eric Carle's book, *Mr Seahorse*.

As the children arrive, they hang up their coats, complete a register, wander to their friends, and venture to various areas of the classroom. Ellie and Tom meet in the role-play area. The children in the class decided at the beginning of term that this area would be based on the theme of 'the deep blue sea'. The corner is decorated with hangings made from pieces of material brushed with watery colours, from blue and turquoise dye, and sprinklings of piped silver, raised textile paint. There are sea creature-shaped collages embellished with brightly coloured papers and sequins. A5 pieces of paper, strung together with ribbon, hang down and shimmer with painted colours of the sand and the sea. The sea colours have been applied with thick powder paints, where children have added flour and experimented with lines of patterns in water. Meanwhile the sand palettes have an array of yellows, from ochre to lemon. They indicate previous experiments with texture, which include sand, rice, mini shells, and glue, with shimmering additions of thick gold paint. On the floor lies a woven piece of netting, involving a range of ribbons and textured threads, including metallic, fluorescent and PVC, in a range of blue and gold. Tom sits with a small doll and Ellie searches for a 'Mr Seahorse'. Around them hang small painted sea creatures cut into different shapes from salt dough and strung on coloured ribbons. A small water feature fountain is turned on and the water trickles as they begin to play 'underwater families'.

From 'The Deep Blue Sea' case study you will begin to recognise the opportunities available in classrooms for linking materials to visual elements. By doing so, teachers engage children in an ongoing process of visual, spatial and tactile development. Children are brought into contact with the range of visual, spatial and tactile elements, through experiences which involve looking, touching and talking. This forms part of an education in art and design, where children become aware of, and alert to, the visual, spatial and tactile diversity of the world.

By making connections to materials and artistic experiences and processes, children are increasingly able to apply this awareness to making and thinking about art and design itself. They are able to explore and represent ideas, feelings and impulses by combining materials and visual qualities; children become visually literate. Good art and design teaching supports this, and helps children to develop as visually articulate young people.

PRACTICAL TASK PRACTICAL TASK PRACTICAL TASK PRACTICAL TASK PRACTICAL TASK

Read 'The Deep Blue Sea' case study and identify the visual, tactile and spatial elements; identify which materials support these elements. Think about and identify how children, by creating this role-play area, have developed as visually articulate and aware young people. Keep in mind that expressions of this form of literacy are evident in the objects and images of art and design, and in the spoken and written word.

Knowledge and understanding of materials and processes

The National Curriculum (DfEE, 1999) describes knowledge and understanding of materials and processes as including:

- drawing;
- painting;
- printmaking;
- collage;
- textiles;
- sculpture;
- digital media.

To develop your understanding of these areas of learning in art and design, here, and throughout this book, we are describing these as *'experiences'*. These experiences have associated materials and processes. (We have made this decision to avoid confusion with the processes of learning which include explore, develop, investigate, make, review and evaluate, see *Chapter 3: Considering learners and learning: principles and practice*.)

For example, a drawing experience might involve the following:

Experience: drawing

Materials: pencils, colour pencils, felt pens, water soluble pencils, oil pastels, chalk pastels, pens, fine line pens, marker pens, threads, string, rope, torn and cut paper, masking tape, plastic insulating tape.

Processes: hold, control, apply, make marks, repeat, modify, investigate, explore.

To make sense of the progressive nature of experiences and their related materials and processes they are presented through this section in 'chart' form. You will be able to identify how processes and materials constitute the experiences, and how experiences involve skill development and application (see pp67–71, Figures 4.5–4.9).

Knowledge and understanding of areas of experience is built through activity, reflection and evaluation, and supported by engagement with the work of artists, craftspeople and designers, and by making connections to visual, tactile and spatial elements. This approach encourages areas of learning to be seen as interlinked and co-dependent.

Beyond the experiences detailed in the charts, we have developed drawing and ICT and digital media, as areas of learning which support and develop other areas, as well as being discrete art and design activities and experiences.

Drawing

Although technological and cultural change continues to alter the appearance of some artistic practices, for many artists, craftspeople and designers drawing remains a significant and central activity. In some cases drawings are presented as finished art works: framed, hung on walls, projected on screens, or folded into books. In other cases drawing is a key part of the exploration, research, development and investigation process; drawings are made by hand or with mechanical or digital tools, resulting in buildings, cars, suits, chairs, sculpture and jewellery.

In primary school drawing can take a similarly diverse role, as a central feature of art and design curriculum activities, or as a tool for enquiry across the curriculum. In a similar way to artists, children value drawing as a significant and varied activity. Drawing serves a range of purposes and takes on a whole raft of appearances, from visual diaries of 'growing beans', to imaginary worlds of underwater adventure, from carefully observed patterns in brickwork, to 'mental maps' of local journeys.

Children willingly engage in drawing activities from a very early age when they make and organise marks to explore observations, ideas and feelings or generate new ones. They make drawings on many occasions with little or limited direction from teachers or other adults, during lessons, at home, during wet play times, on the playground and in corridors, on scrap paper, in sketchbooks, or on top of photographs.

For adults and children drawing is a means of graphically exploring, explaining and inventing through meaningful marks, as such drawings vary in type and appearance dependent on intention and materials used.

Drawings involve organising meaningful marks:	Drawing marks imply:	Drawings encourage:	Drawings appear as:	Drawing materials include:
Lines	Age	Analysis	Animations	
Curves	Character	Communication	Annotated	Pens
Dots	Contour	Comparison	sketches	Pencils
Shapes	Distance	Creation	Bird's eye views	Coloured pens
Splodges	Direction	Decoration	Contour	Coloured pencils
Cross-hatching	Division	Detail	drawings	Felt pens
Hatching	Enclosure	Discovery	Designs	Charcoal
Shading	Edge	Embellishment	Doodles	Crayon
Patterns	Form	Expression	Diagrams	Marker pens
Points	Grandeur	Exploration	Extended	Chalk
Rhythmically	Location	Evaluation	photographs	Wet hands on
Organically	Mood	Examination	Fold-out	dry surfaces
Hesitantly	Movement	Invention	illustrations	Sticks in sand
Boldly	Place	Knowledge	Maps	Found objects
Sensitively	Position	Looking	Observational	Balls rolled in
Expressively	Pattern	Making	drawings	paint
Slowly	Size	Observation	Outlines	Masking tape
Quickly	Relation	Perception	Overlays	Cut and torn
Geometrically	Route	Recording	Panoramas	paper
Systematically	Scale	Reflection	Plan	Wire
Fluidly	Space	Research	Pop-up	Paint
	Surface	Review	Speed drawings	Light
	Texture	Understanding	Sketches	Rollers and ink
	Time	Wonder	Storyboards	Inks and brushes
			Technical	
			drawings	
			Tracings	
			X-ray sections	

adapted and developed from Adams (2003)

Figure 4.2 Making meaning through drawing

Adams (2004) suggests that by engaging with drawing, by organising meaningful marks, children learn about:

Perception
- Drawing that assists the ordering of sensations, feelings, ideas and thoughts.

'These drawings help children understand both the external world of people, objects and events as well the inner world of feelings, desires and imaginings. Here their drawings might not make sense to anyone else. It does not matter, as long as they help children make sense of their world.'

Adams, (2004, p6)

Communication
- Drawing that assists the process of making ideas, thoughts and feelings available to others.
- The audience may be known, it may be part of a group activity, discussion or interaction.

'... the intention might be to communicate ideas. Here it is necessary to draw in a way that the viewer will understand. Each area of the curriculum has its own set of codes and conventions (graphs, charts, timelines, maps)... Annotated sketches are useful for every curriculum area, linking both visual information and verbal explanation.'

Adams, (2004, p6)

Invention
- Drawing that assists the creative manipulation and development of thought.

'Sometimes it is too difficult to try to work out something just by sitting and thinking about it. Drawing can act as prompt to thought, helping to spark new ideas and connections. Where children have been allowed to experiment, to play with ideas without fear of failure, this has given rise to a greater variety of possibilities. They learn to turn their so-called mistakes into something else.'

Adams, (2004, p6)

All these activities require a range of skills developed through the exploration and control of a variety of tools, and skills of observation. 'Making marks is a natural ability. Drawing is not. Drawing is making marks that have meaning. It is something that we learn to do. Drawing helps children learn how to learn, to organise information, to express ideas and to shape their thinking. Encouraging children to draw will improve their confidence and skill as learners'.

Adams (2004, p6)

Information Communication Technology (ICT) and digital media

The National Society for Education in Art and Design (NSEAD) (2009) suggest:

In art and design education the use of computers, scanners, digital cameras, printers and the Internet is challenging us to rethink the ways in which we develop pupils' creativity. ICT blurs the boundary between traditional art and design forms providing opportunities to express ideas in many different ways. In teaching art and design we need to consider how ICT might be used alongside and or integrated with art and design practice and how to develop this new medium in a way that develops and extends visual understanding.

(NSEAD, 2009)

The provision of positive ICT experiences in art and design is not consistently widespread. Some schools engage children in exciting projects employing digital media to produce animations, videos or soundscapes. Other schools have more limited activity, restricting opportunities to using digital cameras to record and document projects. As you make decisions to support learning in art and design you will be able to consider the benefits of using ICT resources. You will be able to consider the possibilities of centring a project in digital media. The NSEAD (2009) suggest four broad objectives which will help you in this decision making:

How can ICT help pupils' learning in art and design?

- *by enhancing their ability to explore, develop and present ideas*
- *by providing a new medium to investigate and make art and design, craft and design*
- *by providing a tool to evaluate and develop work*
- *by providing access to a range of resources to increase pupils' knowledge and understanding of art and design and design.*

(NSEAD, 2009)

Possible ICT resources	Supporting learning in art and design
Desktop and Laptop PC Data projector Sound recording device Digital camera Digital video camera Digital microscopes Overhead projector DVD player Digital scanner Printer Photocopier Fax machine Mobile phone Internet access Digital galleries Software packages Interactive whiteboard	• Collect and store images and develop in an electronic sketchbook • Select, edit, copy and manipulate digital images • Investigate visual qualities with digital microscopes • Enlarge and repeat images on photocopiers • Present images as a slide show • Select, sequence and edit sound, to produce sound tracks for slide show • Project images into unusual spaces around school • Upload images to school website • Visit a virtual gallery • Make evaluative notes using interactive whiteboard against artists work • Scan and copy drawings to produce multiple images • Project drawings as a back drop to dance performance

Figure 4.3 Using ICT to support learning in art and design

The NSEAD (2009) make further suggestions for art and design activities by suggesting 'cameo' activities and lessons. These offer a purposeful and positive approach to integrating new and traditional technologies.

Each of the cameos in this section highlights an activity which might contribute to a pupil's entitlement to ICT in art and design. Schools will need to review and adapt any activities, including those below, to suit the age, ability and experience of their pupils.

Cameo 1: Exploring and developing ideas
Pupils use a digital video camera to record different viewpoints of pupils in the school environment. They edit their images to create a short film that evokes a sense of mystery. They develop their ideas using a range of traditional media to develop a painting or print based on the work of the surrealists.

Cameo 2: Investigate and make art and design, craft and design
Pupils create designs of their own mythical creatures as part of a topic on the Greeks. Their designs are scanned and modified by applying textures to the creature forms. The completed creature designs are cut out and pasted on to scenes from the local environment.

Cameo 3: Evaluating and developing work
Pupils create a series of digital images and could develop their own class art gallery on the school website.

Cameo 4: Knowledge and understanding
Pupils use the internet to access information on how artists have interpreted the theme of movement.

(NSEAD, 2009)

Figure 4.4 Art and design ICT activities: Key Stage 2

PRACTICAL TASK PRACTICAL TASK **PRACTICAL TASK** PRACTICAL TASK **PRACTICAL TASK**

Make a note of the four 'broad objectives' identified by NSEAD (2009) described under the heading, *How can ICT help pupils' learning in art and design?*

Read the cameo activities detailed above and identify where they meet the 'broad objectives' for ICT and art and design.

Figures 4.5–4.9 provide detailed progression of experiences, materials and processes for drawing and painting, printmaking, collage, textiles and sculpture. These areas form the core activities of art and design in the primary school and where taught should:

- develop from a range of starting points;
- encourage children to work on their own and collaboratively, and on different scales;
- develop a broad range of experiences, material use and awareness of processes;
- explore the work of artists, craftspeople and designers, working in different times and cultures, in a variety of genres, styles and traditions.

(DfEE, 1999, p121)

The following charts are indicative of the progressive experiences to be encouraged in primary art and design. The charts indicate key stage age groups to determine different learning expectations and activities. However, when teaching, it will be useful to consider learners' needs, rather than only key stage or age group, to determine appropriate learning experiences.

Drawing and painting

Early Years Foundation Stage	Key Stage 1	Key Stage 2
Children should be taught to . . . – explore and investigate marks and colour; – hold and control a variety of media and use them to make and repeat various marks and lines; – use lines to create shapes, patterns and textures; – experiment with and apply paint; – notice different colour and tonal qualities; – name, choose and match primary and secondary colours; – describe people, objects, events and places in drawings and paintings; – use simple art and design language related to drawing and painting; – identify and talk about artists' drawings and paintings, recognising colour, line, shape, and pattern.	**Children should be taught to . . .** – recognise and understand qualities of marks and colour in drawings and paintings; – explore and control an increasing variety of media, name them and begin to predict the results that they might achieve; – use lines and marks to create an increasing range of shapes, patterns and textures; – experiment with and control consistency and application of paint; – mix and match colours and make them lighter or darker; – name primary, secondary and some tertiary colours and refer to their hue and tonal value e.g. 'a dark golden yellow'; – make drawings and paintings to show increasing detail and context; – use language to describe visual and tactile qualities of drawings and paintings; – recognise differences and similarities in a range of artists' drawings and paintings.	**Children should be taught to . . .** – apply knowledge of marks and colour to drawings and paintings; – use and control more specialist media to explore ways in which they can be applied to achieve particular effects; – adapt and apply colours to vary hue and tonal range, develop decoration and pattern, and create texture; – match the materials and approach to the scale of work; – compose work and consider the use of available space; – apply knowledge of proportion, scale, ratio and simple perspective; – apply knowledge of visual qualities of work; – describe what has been achieved and how it was produced using art and design vocabulary, including visual qualities; – relate their work to the work of other artists and describe how drawings and paintings could have been made, using art and design vocabulary.
Children should experience . . . – making drawings and paintings from observation, experience and imagination with the emphasis on first-hand experience; – an increasing range of media appropriate to their developing motor co-ordination and control; – drawing and painting on a range of surfaces and scales; – drawing and painting for a range of purposes; – having the opportunity to choose the subject and content of the work; – observing and drawing the human figure in a range of circumstances; – looking at and talking about the work of other artists involved in painting and drawing.	**Children should experience . . .** – making drawings and paintings from observation, experience and imagination with the emphasis on first-hand experience; – drawing for different purposes using a range of styles; – selecting materials and deciding how they might be used; – working on a range of surfaces and scales; – selecting the scale and surface appropriate to the work; – observing and drawing the human figure in a range of active and passive situations; – looking at a wide range of drawings and paintings by artists, and relating them to their own work.	

Figure 4.5 Progression of experiences: drawing and painting

Printmaking

Early Years Foundation Stage	Key Stage 1	Key Stage 2
Children should be taught to ... – explore and investigate transfer and resist methods of printmaking; – recognise printmaking as the transfer or resistance of an image from one surface to another; – load an object with paint or ink and print from it; – print from a range of objects and surfaces; – make rubbings from textured surfaces; – recognise pattern in natural and man-made objects; – use repeated prints to generate patterns; – use simple art and design language related to printmaking; – identify and talk about artists' prints recognising colour, line, shape and pattern.	**Children should be taught to ...** – recognise and understand qualities of transfer and resist prints; – control the amount of paint or ink needed to load a range of objects, and print from them; – make a simple printing block from polystyrene printing tiles or similar; – ink up a block and print a regular and irregular pattern; – apply pressure to control print; – use stencils and other materials as a 'resist' printing method; – use language to describe visual and tactile qualities of prints: line, pattern, texture, shape; – recognise differences and similarities in a range of artists' prints.	**Children should be taught to ...** – apply knowledge of transfer and resist prints; – make a complex relief printing block using a variety of materials; – control line and marks in polystyrene printing tiles to make a two-colour relief print; – ink up a block and print a regular and irregular pattern; – adjust and apply appropriate amounts of ink and pressure to prints; – apply knowledge of repetition, tessellation and symmetry to pattern making; – print to paper and fabric; – use technology to explore and create printed patterns; – describe what has been achieved and how it was produced using art and design vocabulary, including visual qualities; – relate their work to the work of other artists and describe how these prints should have been made, using art and design vocabulary.
Children should experience ... – experimenting with a growing range of printing methods; – choosing objects from which to print to achieve specific results; – printing to make pictures, patterns and/or textures; – printing regular and irregular patterns; – working on a range of surfaces and scales; – creating printed patterns and textures for collage; – identifying and talking about pattern and texture in natural and made objects; – looking at and talking about the work of other artists involved in printmaking.		**Children should experience ...** – experimenting with and combining a range of printing methods; – choosing objects with which to print to achieve specific results; – developing prints to show use of line, pattern and texture; – printing to make pictures, patterns or textures; – printing more complex regular and irregular patterns; – collecting and describing printmaking patterns and textures; – working on a range of scales and surfaces, including fabric; – designing and creating printed patterns and textures for collage; – looking at a wide range of prints made by artists, and relating them to their own work.

Figure 4.6 Progression of experiences: printmaking

Collage

Early Years Foundation Stage	Key Stage 1	Key Stage 2
Children should be taught to . . . – explore and investigate selecting, manipulating and combining collage materials; – hold scissors and cut a range of materials; – cut straight lines; – tear paper into strips and simple shapes; – change the surface of materials by cutting, sticking or tearing; – apply adhesive sparingly and place glued surfaces together accurately; – select and classify materials into shapes, textures and colours; – organise and combine shapes, textures and colours to make pictures or decorative surfaces; – use simple art and design language related to collage; – identify and talk about artists' collages.	**Children should be taught to . . .** – recognise and understand selecting, manipulating and combining collage materials; – cut straight and curved lines from a range of materials with some accuracy; – tear paper into strips and shapes with some accuracy; – manipulate the surface of materials e.g. crumpling, creasing, folding, pleating, scoring, tearing, fraying; – apply adhesive sparingly to a range of materials and place glued surfaces together accurately; – select and classify materials into shapes, textures and colours; – organise and combine shapes, textures and colours as required to make pictures or decorative surfaces; – use language to describe visual and tactile qualities of collages e.g. colour, shape, texture, pattern; – recognise differences and similarities in a range of artists' collages.	**Children should be taught to . . .** – apply knowledge of selecting, manipulating and combining collage materials; – accurately cut complex shapes from a range of materials; – use more specialist cutting equipment and adhesives; – tear paper to predetermined strips and shapes; – alter and manipulate a range of surfaces to create new surfaces appropriate to work; – apply adhesive sparingly and place glued surfaces together accurately; – select materials, shapes and textures for purpose; – edit and combine materials for purpose; – describe what has been achieved and how it was produced using art and design vocabulary, including visual qualities; – relate their work to the work of other artists and describe how these collages could have been made, using art and design vocabulary.
Children should experience . . . – handling and manipulating a wide range of natural and made materials and making choices to match texture and colour to purpose; – making their own collage choosing and applying various coloured, shaped, textured and patterned materials; – creating new materials for collage, by cutting, manipulating and combining existing materials; – talk about their work and the work of others and use language appropriate to the visual qualities of shape, texture and colour; – work as a member of a group producing a single collage; – looking at and talking about the work of other artists involved in collage.		**Children should experience . . .** – planning and producing their own collage, choosing, cutting, arranging and applying materials, focusing on colour, shape, texture and pattern; – experimenting further with materials to achieve new surfaces for collage; – talking about their work and the work of others, using language appropriate to visual qualities and identifying how artists select, manipulate and combine materials; – looking at a wide range of collages made by artists, and relating them to their own work.

Figure 4.7 Progression of experiences: collage

Textiles		
Early Years Foundation Stage	Key Stage 1	Key Stage 2
Children should be taught to... – explore and investigate threads and fabrics, stitching and weaving; – collect and classify fabrics and threads into colours and different textures; – hold scissors and cut fabrics and threads; – thread beads onto a lace or string; – combine and stick fabrics and threads together; – weave materials through open-weave surfaces e.g. plastic webbing, plastic fencing; – dye a range of fabrics and threads; – use simple art and design language related to textiles; – identify and talk about artists' textile work.	**Children should be taught to...** – recognise and understand qualities of fabrics and threads, including stitching and weaving; – cut fabric carefully into shapes; – cut threads into a variety of similar lengths; – sort and classify fabrics and threads by colour and texture; – thread a large-eyed needle; – sew individual straight stitches as decoration on suitable open-weave fabrics; – dye a range of fabrics and threads for collage purposes; – weave with paper and card on a warp made from smooth threads; – use language to describe visual and tactile qualities of textiles, e.g. texture, surface; – recognise differences and similarities in a range of artists' textile work.	**Children should be taught to...** – apply knowledge of fabrics and threads, including stitching and weaving to textile work; – cut and apply fabrics and threads with accuracy; – create and apply new fabric textures, e.g. crumpling, creasing and pleating; – create new threads by, for example, knotting and plaiting, to use as decoration; – thread and sew with fine metal needles; – sew with straight stitches to create patterns and surface decoration; – sew pieces of fabric together accurately using the sewing machine and/or by hand; – weave using a wide range of fabric strips and threads; – create patterns in fabric as a result of dyeing; – cut a simple paper pattern and use it to create a basic 3D shape from fabric; – describe what has been achieved and how it was produced using art and design vocabulary, including visual qualities; – relate their work to the textile work of other artists and describe how these could have been made, using art and design vocabulary.
Children should experience... – handling and manipulating a wide range of fabrics and threads; – selecting fabrics and threads for collage purposes in terms of colour and texture; – wrapping dolls and other shapes in fabrics; – dressing themselves and talking about fastenings and different fabrics; – simple sewing to create a surface texture or pattern on fabric; – weaving to create textures and patterns; – dyeing threads and fabrics that will be used in other textile activities; – looking at and talking about the work of other artists involved in textiles.	**Children should experience...** – planning and creating 2D collages and 3D structures using fabrics and threads and combining previously learned techniques as appropriate to the work; – selecting fabrics and threads to support the purpose of the work; – weaving to create textures and patterns; – tie-dyeing fabrics to achieve patterns and textures and to achieve particular effects required by the work; – experimenting with techniques to achieve effects that are appropriate to the work; – looking at a wide range of textiles made by artists, and relating them to their own work.	

Figure 4.8 Progression of experiences: textiles

Sculpture

Early Years Foundation Stage	Key Stage 1	Key Stage 2
Children should be taught to... – explore and investigate plastic, rigid and semi-rigid 3D materials; – mould and create simple shapes with malleable materials, e.g. dough; – assemble and disassemble component parts of a range of construction kits; – combine boxes and other found materials to create junk models; – use simple tools to cut, shape and impress patterns and textures in a range of materials; – develop the language to describe structures achieved; – use simple art and design language related to sculpture; – identify and talk about artists' sculpture.	**Children should be taught to...** – recognise and understand joining, combining, adding and reducing, to form structures in sculpture; – mould malleable materials, e.g. clay, to create objects and people from a range of component shapes; – use simple techniques for building and joining clay; – use a wider range of simple tools to cut, shape and impress patterns and textures in a range of materials; – create simple shapes from paper and card, and other rigid materials; – create papier-mâché and use it to model 3D shapes; – make plaster casts; – use language to describe visual, tactile and spatial qualities of sculpture e.g. form, space, shape; – recognise differences and similarities in a range of artists' sculptures.	**Children should be taught to...** – apply knowledge of joining, combining, adding and reducing to sculptural objects; – shape and impress pattern and texture with intention and accuracy; – manipulate and combine rigid materials to form upright, balanced and spanning structures; – create forms from semi-rigid materials with intention and accuracy; – use plaster to create relief surfaces; – describe what has been achieved and how it was produced using art and design vocabulary, including visual qualities; – relate their work to the sculpture of other artists and describe how these could have been made, using art and design vocabulary.

Children should experience...
– building and constructing structures from a wide range of materials and objects;
– working on a range of scales and sizes;
– combining materials and processes to achieve required effects and meet specific design requirements, for example in the production of a large figure involving an armature, the building of the body and its decoration;
– working with specific malleable (especially clay) and resistant materials to explore their qualities;
– planning the sculpture and selecting appropriate materials and tools to work with;
– looking at and talking about the work of other artists involved in sculpture.

Children should experience...
– building and constructing structures from a wide range of materials and objects;
– working on a range of scales and sizes;
– combining materials and processes to achieve required effects and meet specific design requirements, for example in the production of a large figure involving an armature, the building of the body and its decoration;
– working with specific malleable (especially clay) and resistant materials to explore their qualities;
– planning the sculpture and selecting appropriate materials and tools to work with;
– looking at a wide range of sculpture made by artists and relating them to their own work.

Figure 4.9 Progression of experiences: sculpture

Knowledge and understanding of artists, craftspeople and designers

The requirement to consider and learn about the work of artists, craftspeople and designers has been present in some form in the different versions of the National Curriculum. It provides an opportunity to address a curricular imbalance that for many years focused almost exclusively on making. Children are encouraged to investigate the work of others to support their:

1. developing art and design activity;
2. increasingly alert visual, tactile and spatial awareness;
3. awareness of artistic practices as culturally significant activities.

By looking at and investigating the work of artists, craftspeople, and designers, children can see the graphic, decorative, spatial, or tactile solutions arrived at by others. In this way children can be taught about these solutions as possible starting points for developing and enhancing their own work.

For example children *develop their own art and design* by:

- learning about drawing solutions by comparing artists' work;
- making applications of paint and examining painterly approaches to brush work;
- developing solutions for occupying public spaces with sculpture by looking at monuments and buildings;
- examining approaches to decorating and embellishing objects by looking at a range of contemporary craftspeople;
- using line and mark to articulate movement and speed by comparing artists;
- exploring strategies used by artists to create illusions of depth;
- looking at approaches used by architects to develop and explore ideas to create imaginative furniture.

Unfortunately, school-based approaches have tended to focus on a fairly narrow and predictable range of artists, craftspeople and designers. A challenge for you will be to draw on your own experience and expand your awareness of artists to cover what the National Curriculum (DfEE, 1999) describes as artists, craftspeople and designers *working in different times and cultures, in a variety of genres, styles and traditions*.

To support the use of more diverse artists, craftspeople and designers it may be useful to take a theme-based approach, making use of the suggested genres (or themes as described by Taylor, 1998), styles and traditions. Although there is some interplay between these terms, and the National Curriculum offers no further detail, they are certainly useful starting points.

Figure 4.10 is far from exhaustive, with a focus on the twentieth century, and an interpretation of what can be considered as genre or tradition. However, working within and across these themes provides a number of benefits:

1. comparisons can be made to identify similarities and differences;
2. the similarities and differences reflect different contexts of time and place;
3. awareness of contextual significance can be developed.

Traditions of making art	Possible genres or themes	Possible styles or movements or periods
Painting Drawing Printmaking Collage Montage Textiles Sculpture Installation Video Sound Photography	Landscape Environment Objects Still life Narrative Events Portrait Self-portrait Human figure Fantasy Representation Identity	Impressionist Expressionist Cubist Surrealist Constructivist Abstract-expressionist Pop Minimalist Optical Kinetic Photo realist Performance Conceptual

Figure 4.10 Examples of genre, tradition and style

PRACTICAL TASK PRACTICAL TASK PRACTICAL TASK PRACTICAL TASK PRACTICAL TASK

Identify an artist, designer or craftsperson with whose work you are familiar. Collect an image of their work. Identify a tradition and genre for the work, and if appropriate a style or movement – the date of the work may help you with this process. Research and compare an artist, craftsperson or designer, who works with a similar genre or theme but from a different style or tradition. For example, the Tate Modern curated its initial gallery spaces by themes. In one room a Richard Long image was mirrored with a painting by Claude Monet. Separated by almost one hundred years, and producing work with many differences, similarities were also evident. Both artists could be seen to be working in the traditions of 'landscape'.

To support children with sustained engagement with works by artists, craftspeople and designers, and to set the work in historical and social contexts, many teachers adopt 'models' as 'ways into work'. Although these models vary (Taylor, 1986; Buchanan, 1995; Addison, 2000) they usually rely on a process of *description, interpretation and some evaluation.* They provide useful frameworks for looking, which build from empirical study, describing and discussing what can be seen or experienced, and extended with further reference to artefacts or texts.

PRACTICAL TASK PRACTICAL TASK PRACTICAL TASK PRACTICAL TASK PRACTICAL TASK

Examples of artists who explore drawing.

- Charles Avery
- William Blake
- Vija Celmins
- Chuck Close
- Helen Frankenthaler
- David Hockney

- William Kentridge
- Henri Matisse
- Vincent van Gogh.

Select two artists from the 'drawing' list. Find examples of their drawings and stick them on a page, annotate the drawings using vocabulary from Figure 4.10 to describe and compare their work.

Visit Drumcroon's web site (www.drumcroon.org) and navigate to the teaching materials for *Pupils as Critics* (KS3), found in the *Projects* area. Use the prompts in the 'writing frames' to extend your annotations, following the suggested areas of *content, process, form and mood* (Taylor, 1986).

Compile lists of artists against each of the other artistic experiences.

- painting
- printmaking
- collage
- textiles
- sculpture
- digital media.

CASE STUDY

Mrs McCarthy, the Year 3 teacher at Pemberton Junior School, visited the Byzantium Exhibition at the Royal Academy in London during the school vacation. Inspired by many of the exhibits and artefacts on display, she intends to adapt her planning to incorporate some of the ideas. She aims to blend some of the historical facts and the stimulus from Constantine into her Roman project. She will consider what happened after the Roman Empire, and will adapt a one-off lesson inspired by some of the metal 'repoussé' mark making. Using copper foil children will use pencils to draw patterns inspired from different Byzantium images and combine them with Roman patterns. The intention is to display the small pieces of copper as a collaborative museum exhibit.

REFLECTIVE TASK

Read the case study above. Mrs McCarthy is comfortable with the opportunities found in museum or gallery settings. She is prepared to extend her experience and knowledge of art and design by engaging in cultural activities and events.

Consider how you will support your development needs, with reference to the *continuum of experience, needs, confidence and support* detailed in the Introduction and developed in *Chapter 5: Considering teachers and teaching: principles*. Complete the following art and design subject knowledge and understanding audit. Identify action to support your needs: visit a gallery, refer to publications, visit websites, explore art and design materials, listen to teachers, and listen to pupils.

Area of knowledge and understanding	Introductory level	Threshold level	Post-threshold level
Visual, tactile and spatial elements	Review:	Review:	Action:
	Review:	Action:	Action:
Experiences, materials and processes	Review:	Review:	Action:
	Review:	Action:	Action:
ICT and digital media	Review:	Review:	Action:
	Review:	Action:	Action:
Artists, craftspeople and designers	Review:	Review:	Action:
	Review:	Action:	Action:

Figure 4.11 Art and design subject knowledge and understanding audit

Providing a broad and balanced curriculum experience for children will support learning in art and design. Dedicating learning opportunities to particular areas of knowledge or understanding will support more considered art and design activity. In this way children will be able to draw from an increasingly broad and developed range and repertoire of artistic experiences, and make connections to their visual, tactile and spatial development. Children's inventive and purposeful art and design activity will reflect knowledge and understanding, as children articulate their ideas in ever more visually and spatially articulate ways.

A SUMMARY OF **KEY POINTS**

This chapter has developed and extended your understanding of:

> **learning in primary art and design;**

> **the importance of visual, tactile and spatial elements in developing visually and spatially articulate young children;**

> **the role of starting points and vocabulary in developing visual, tactile and spatial enquiry;**

> **the range of experiences, materials and processes relevant to primary art and design;**

> **the opportunities provided through engagement with the work of artists, craftspeople and designers.**

MOVING *ON* > > > **> > >** MOVING *ON* > > > **> > >** MOVING *ON*

Continue to extend your visual, tactile and spatial awareness, keep your senses open and alert to your environment. Make visual notes in a sketchbook, take photographs, and collect examples of work by artists, craftspeople and designers. Begin to see and think in artistically sensitive ways, and consider ways of engaging children with similar experiences.

REFERENCES REFERENCES **REFERENCES** REFERENCES **REFERENCES** REFERENCES

Adams, E (2003) *Start drawing*. Drawing Power, The Campaign for Drawing.

Adams, E (2004) Why draw? *Start*, Corsham: NSEAD, No. 7, 2004.

Addison, N (2000) Critical and contextual studies, in Addison, N and Burgess, L (eds) *Learning to teach art and design in the secondary school*. Abingdon: RoutledgeFalmer.

Bowden, J (2006) *The primary art and design subject leader's handbook*. Corsham: NSEAD.

Buchanan, M (1995) Making art and critical literacy: A reciprocal relationship, in Prentice, R (ed) *Teaching art and design*. London: Cassell.

DfEE (1999) *The National Curriculum*. London: HMSO.

DCSF (2008) *Early Years Foundation Stage Statutory Framework*. Nottingham: DCSF Publications.

www.drumcroon.org.uk/School%20Projects/projects.html (accessed, May 2009).

www.nsead.org/ict/index.aspx (accessed May, 2009).

Taylor, R (1986) *Educating for art*. Harlow: Longman.

Taylor, R (1998) *Understanding and investigating art: Bringing the National Gallery into the art room*. London: Hodder & Stoughton.

FURTHER READING FURTHER READING **FURTHER READING** FURTHER READING

Adams, E (2003) *Start drawing*. Drawing Power, The Campaign for Drawing.

Adams, E (2003) *Power drawing*. Drawing Power, The Campaign for Drawing.

Adams, E (2004) *Space and place*. Drawing Power, The Campaign for Drawing.

Anning, A and Ring, K (2004) *Making sense of children's drawings*. Maidenhead: Open University Press/McGraw-Hill.

Charman, H, Rose, C and Wilson, G (eds) (2006) *The art gallery handbook: A resource for teachers*. London: Tate.

Fabian, M (2005) *Drawing is a class act: A skills-based approach to drawing*. Dunstable: Brilliant Publications.

Websites

www.artisancamnorth.org.uk

A fascinating site, full of inspiration, workshops, activities, artists talking, children working.

www.dareonline.org

Digital Art Resource for Education: a thematically-organised site of contemporary artists' work: play, space and place, translation.

www.drawingpower.org.uk

Exciting national developments involving drawing.

www.drumcroon.org.uk/About/aboutus.html

Drumcroon is an art education centre in Wigan. It has pioneered approaches to art and design with children and this website reflects the diversity of its work.

www.nsead.org/primary/resources/mags.aspx

Links to a range of galleries and museums

5
Considering teachers and teaching: principles

Chapter objectives

By the end of this chapter you will have:

- **broadened your awareness and understanding of the nature of art and design teaching;**
- **developed your awareness of the role and identity of the art and design teacher;**
- **developed an awareness of your self as a potential teacher of art and design.**

This chapter addresses the following Standards for QTS: **Q1, Q7, Q8, Q10, Q14**.

Key themes: emerging identities; confidence; continuum; teaching and artistry; the artist teacher; teacher interventions; support and challenge; intervention and observation; professional understanding; traditions.

Introduction

The pattern of chapters to this point has encouraged you to think about primary art and design along the following lines.

- What is required and how it is rationalised: Chapter 1
- What may be possible, by thinking of children as creative artists: Chapter 2
- How and what children learn: Chapter 3
- How learning can be described and organised: Chapter 4

This chapter encourages you to think 'how things may be taught'. Ultimately we are hopeful that you will find a way of teaching art and design that is meaningful and worthwhile; for yourself and for children. This chapter aims to help you towards this point, by acknowledging the ebb and flow of your emerging teacher identity. There will be times when you feel confident and assured about what you are aiming to teach, and at other times you may feel less confident. You will find security from working closely with colleagues or peers, and with lesson ideas which feel comfortable or familiar. The message explored through this chapter suggests that if you can see yourself along a continuum of change and development, upon which you can move backwards and forwards, matching your confidence or otherwise to the situation in which you find yourself, you will be in a good position to develop as a teacher. This position will go some way to enabling you to act in ways which help you secure appropriate teaching relationships with children. To encourage your thinking within this reflective process, the chapter includes a range of portraits of art and design teachers. In addition, their characteristics and approaches to teaching will be described in the context of other educational ideas and themes. From these you will be able to make connections and comparisons with your emerging identity, helping with the reflective and critical approach to becoming a teacher.

Influences on teaching art and design

Influences which start with children

CASE STUDY 5.1

PORTRAIT 1: MRS ADAMS

At the beginning of the Year 2 art and design lesson Mrs Adams is sitting on the carpeted area of the classroom, holding a number of books and looking relaxed as children make an organised circle around her. She begins reading from one of the books. The selected passage describes the movements of a dancer and of a football player, using a poetic language of grace, beauty, balance, rhythm and speed.

The children listen carefully. They are then asked to close their eyes. Mrs Adams reads the passage again, and this time she asks the children to imagine, or call up from their minds, people dancing and playing football. The passage is then developed into a recollection of a previous physical education lesson where the children followed movement patterns echoing the flow of movements in a number of sports.

Set out on each table is a range of drawing and painting materials: coloured pencils, water colour paint sets, pencils and oil pastels, assorted brushes and pots of clean water, and large sheets of white cartridge paper.

Mrs Adams encourages the class to think about painting a picture to capture the rhythms of the dancers or football players, in shapes of bold colour. She reminds the children that their own ideas are the ones which really matter, asking them to be confident in expressing themselves through the variety of materials, and to enjoy the activity. Finally she reminds the class to be respectful of the classroom environment and to exercise some care when moving around with materials and resources.

In the early part of the twentieth century much of the initial interest in children's imagery was taken up by practising artists. In the early 1990s, during a time of rapid change in contemporary western art, often referred to as 'modernism', a number of artists found themselves drawn to the art of children. In the work of children, these artists observed a sense of freedom, imaginative creative responses and what were thought of as *unique* artistic expressions. For example, for the artist Kandinsky the value of child art was clear:

> *Children are not worried about conventional and practical meanings, since they look at the world with unspoiled eyes and are able to experience things as they are effortlessly... Thus, without exception, every child's drawing reveals the* inner *sound of objects.*
>
> (Kandinsky, in Wilson, 1992, p18)

Similar observations made by artists, and increasingly those involved in education, led to an exploration of the possibility of 'child art'. The argument for 'child art' was one centred on the child, on their imaginative responses, their creative energies and output, on individual well-being, and on art as a vehicle for expression. One such advocate of the educational benefits of child-centred art, was the influential Marion Richardson. Writing in 1948 and reflecting on her early days in teaching, Richardson promotes a non-interventionist approach to children and their art making:

I began to see that this thing we had stumbled on...w[as] art not drawing; something as distinct and special and precious as love itself, and as natural. I could free it, but I could not teach it; and my whole purpose was now directed to this end, as I set out to learn with and from the children.

(Richardson, 1948, p13)

Richardson extended her interest in children and art throughout her education career, working in London and Birmingham as a teacher and for the local education authorities. She is regarded as one of the most influential figures in the promotion of 'child art' and art education. It is possibly reassuring that someone of such distinction remained unsure of exactly how to teach. As she suggests, she is willing to learn from children, to preserve the *precious* and the *natural*. In many ways her legacy lives on in schools, and is reflected in Portrait 1. Teachers share her desire to maintain the special qualities of children's art; they seek to preserve children's 'unspoiled eyes'. They would advocate characteristics shared in Portrait 1:

- encouragement
- freedom
- nature
- enjoyment
- individuality
- charisma
- creativity.

Influences which start from the subject of art and design

CASE STUDY 5.2
PORTRAIT 2: MS EVANS

The interactive whiteboard is illuminated with the glowing image of a painting by Sonia Delaunay, and as the class take their seats they are asked to focus on the painting's composition, its shapes and the artist's use of colour. The Year 5 class is divided into smaller groups of four, determined by the existing seating arrangements. They are asked, via a nominated scribe, to record associated words, under the three headings composition, shape and colour. Following a five-minute period, the groups share their thoughts with the class and Ms Evans assembles a class list of vocabulary for this particular painting.

The interactive whiteboard then shows a range of pots of paint, which with the touch of a virtual button can be mixed on screen. Ms Evans demonstrates mixing colours using primary, secondary and complementary colours. A volunteer then steps forward to create their own virtual Delaunay image, mirroring the composition, shapes and colour.

Each table has been provided with a selection of paints, brushes, mixing palettes and clean water. Working in their sketchbooks, the children are asked to produce a palette of colours similar to those used by Delaunay and then to make an image in her 'style'. These activities are reworded and projected on to the whiteboard in the form of learning intentions.

In response to the dominance of the child-centred approach to art and design education, a number of educators became increasingly concerned with the need to promote art and design as a subject or discipline. In other words they were concerned not solely with the wellbeing of individuals, through opportunities for creative self expression, but with the promotion of knowledge, skills, processes and values associated with art and design. *Chapter 4: Knowledge and understanding: progression of experiences and processes* identifies these in detail as currently described in the National Curriculum (DfEE, 1999).

A number of influences resulted in a gradual shift in schools from a child-centred art and design approach, towards a subject-centred approach. In a number of art schools an influential practice referred to as 'basic design' (mirroring practices from the influential Bauhaus approaches to teaching art and design) was advocated. To promote creative artistic responses, students were encouraged to follow a systematic and developmental curriculum. This would provide opportunities for students to develop a visual language (colour, line, pattern, shape, form, tone, space, composition) and to explore a number of artistic practices, drawing, painting, printmaking, via a series of workshops.

This emphasis on an *education in* art became the focus for primary and secondary art and design discussion, both in the United Kingdom and the USA. The result in both cases was strikingly similar, as solutions were proposed to ease the concerns expressed about a heavy diet of child-centred art and design education. Field (1973) comments:

> If the one (child art) focuses attention on the pupil, the latter calls attention to the discipline of art; if the former involves minimal teaching, the latter proclaims there is *material* that needs teaching; if for the former the practice of art is sufficient, the latter calls attention to the claims of aesthetics, criticism and art history. While we were giving full attention to the former, we could hardly heed the latter.
>
> (Field, 1973, p156)

In Field's identification of 'criticism' and 'art history', in addition to the practical aspects of art and design education, it is possible to identify a significant change. Where child art had been universally accepted as revolving around the practical work of children, this new subject focus shifted attention to other artists, craftspeople and designers. Not only did it suggest knowledge about such artists and their work, but asked pupils to reflect on, share and discuss ideas and opinions. Art education was re-conceived as involving action, thought and reflection.

This balance between making and appraising is maintained in the current National Curriculum. Not only was the shift significant in terms of *what* was to be taught, i.e. knowledge of artists from different times and cultures, as well as knowledge and skills associated with techniques and visual qualities, but also in terms of *how* these things were to be taught. The methods of Marion Richardson were seen as outdated and 'laissez faire' (Barnes, 2006, p21). The need to study the work of other artists invigorated many art teachers, and challenged others.

In response, educators committed to the idea of a subject-led approach to art education would advocate the practices seen in Portrait 2:

- support;
- expertise;
- knowledge;
- skills;
- structure;
- reflection;
- culture;
- competence.

REFLECTIVE TASK

REFLECTIVE TASK

The events described in Portraits 1 and 2 provide a clear distinction between approaches in art and design. The lists of words help describe those practices. Write down the lists side by side and add further words to each list. Categorising this way can be useful, but you will notice areas where there is overlap and convergence. From your experiences in school have you seen teachers working in these distinct ways or are the boundaries less obvious? Would you consider one approach more suitable for Key Stage 1 or 2? How would you suggest teachers can work with child-centred ideas within a disciplined approach to the subject? In other words, can you conceive a third approach?

Taken as they are, the two portraits of art and design teachers may appear to present you with a choice of 'either/or'. However, in practice it is common to find teachers operating in both ways, as they shift around in their teaching role. Indeed the National Curriculum itself can be seen to advocate three distinct types of teacher: the *expert*, to teach skills and knowledge, the *facilitator* to encourage investigation and the *philosopher* to engage with discussion and opinion (Hallam, Lee and Gupta, 2007).

Influences which start from art and artistry

CASE STUDY 5.3

PORTRAIT 3: MISS HAMBLE

Sitting at their tables, the children listen carefully as Miss Hamble lists the new groupings for the forthcoming arts week. She explains how groups have been determined from the personal work explored at home, and during wet play times, in their small sketchbooks, throughout the term. The sketchbooks are returned to each group as the class reorganises itself. The personal ideas generated by the Year 4 class from their own sketchbook ideas are classified under four headings: hobbies, people, stories and events. With each heading Miss Hamble offers a pack of images from artists exploring similar themes, as possible ways to develop work.

The challenge for the children, during the mornings of the art week, is to produce work influenced by their own initial sketchbook ideas. Emphasis is placed on the need to work as a group, to share ideas, to work on different scales and to think how different materials might suit any change in scale. The children respond to the challenge with silence. This is followed by a period of busy questions and answers. Miss Hamble has anticipated many of the questions and drawn up a checklist, describing what is considered appropriate to support creative responses to the challenge. It includes a definition of materials that can be used, stored in new art boxes, one per group, access to one computer per group and the use of a number of software packages, explored earlier in the year. The final pieces of the art week will form a gallery, and the process of working will be recorded with a camera, one per group, with further written diary extracts covering the week, recorded initially to digital voice recorders.

Miss Hamble stresses the need to be playful and imaginative; to work like artists. The idea of working as an artist is then supported with video material showing an artist developing their work from initial ideas to finished piece.

In an attempt to offer a further way of approaching and visualising the teacher of primary art and design, our next influence takes its lead from the characteristics of artists, and from art itself. This formation of a teacher may feel a little loose, although echoing some of the attributes heard earlier in the child-centred model, it adopts a more reflective and critical approach to teaching. In a positive sense, this image of a teacher is born out of a fairly straightforward need to think about the role of the teacher, and the relationships they establish with children. You are asked to think about these using language more commonly considered by artists. As we saw earlier, this may involve being:

imaginative	focused	curious	inventive
perceptive	determined	developmental	motivational
reflective	independent	practical	mediawise
collaborative	playful	environmental	thoughtful

Eisner (1985, 2003) is a particularly strong advocate of the benefits of seeing teaching as an art, observing teaching through the lens of the artist and relating to the qualities of *artistry*. He suggests four areas for consideration, areas where teaching shares experiences and commonalities with the arts and the artist, rather than the sciences or the technician.

Teaching and art as a source of aesthetic experience

In a classroom where a teacher operates with grace or beauty, sensitivity or balance, where they operate and construct ideas with dynamism and subtlety, they share an experience akin to the arts. Where teachers demonstrate these traits they can be described with the 'adjectives and accolades usually applied to the fine arts' (Eisner, 1985, p176).

REFLECTIVE TASK

Commit yourself to writing a reflective account of a teaching and learning experience which uses the language of the arts. To do this you will need to develop a vocabulary list, and then be bold, use language which is rarely used when evaluating lessons. This is not easy, but stick with it. Do you find this experience liberating and empowering or does it make you feel nervous and vulnerable?

Teaching and art as involving judgements which unfold during activity

It is currently determined as appropriate to predict before lessons or activities what children will learn during that experience. Eisner suggests an alternative: he is committed not to prediction, but to the emergence and unfolding of ideas. This process is one shared by the painter (or other artist), as they make judgements and decisions based on the developing work. For the teacher to work in a similar way, they need to form particular relationships with pupils and their work, encouraging and 'reading the emerging qualities...In this process qualitative judgement is exercised in achieving a qualitative end' (Eisner, 1985, p176).

PRACTICAL TASK PRACTICAL TASK PRACTICAL TASK PRACTICAL TASK PRACTICAL TASK

Work with a partner. From a single sheet of thin white card, some masking tape, and a small A5 piece of shiny silver paper, produce a number of imaginary plant forms to stand in a small jar. Following the activity, think about how you responded to the materials and to the challenge. How would you go about describing the learning? Did the learning emerge in a similar way to the flowers and plants emerging from the card? Would you be able to predict the learning through decision making before such an activity?

Teaching and art as influenced by the unpredictable

One of the privileges of working in schools is that it is a human activity. Despite fairly non-stop legislation and administrative procedures, its core activity involves young people; by their nature they are unpredictable. Although schools establish rules and systems that in some ways reduce the element of the unpredictable, it is in this slightly risky area that more creative and meaningful events can take place. The teacher needs to be flexible enough to work in such an environment, and robust enough to live with its uncertainty. A 'repertoire' of responses helps navigate these situations, negotiating the unknown and the routine. 'It is precisely the tension between automaticity and inventiveness that makes teaching, like any other art, so complex an undertaking' (Eisner, 1985, p176).

Teaching art as adventure

With the above in mind we can begin to see how the artist and the teacher establish classrooms which encourage adventurous journeys; where outcomes are not always known, or the activities clearly prescribed. It is an exciting and nerve-racking place. In art making emergent ends are sought through a process of enquiry, and this can be translated to the classroom: 'teaching is a form of human action in which many of the ends achieved are emergent' (Eisner, 1985, p176).

PRACTICAL TASK PRACTICAL TASK PRACTICAL TASK PRACTICAL TASK PRACTICAL TASK

Over a period of one week keep a diary, and on each day predict the challenges you will face and how you prepare to overcome them. You could include cooking a meal, getting to a cash machine, finding something to wear, searching for a new camera through the internet. At the end of the day try to pin down how you actually overcame events and challenges, particularly those you didn't predict. What knowledge and skills did you make use of?

When you are asked to plan and prepare for school-based activities does the idea of leaving room for the unpredictable go against your instincts, go against your institutional guidelines for teaching, go against the school's way of working, or do you feel a sense of support in this creative way of working?

It may seem that this artistic description of a teacher sits uncomfortably with many of the constraints of current classroom practice. You would be right, this is a challenging teacher identity, but equally it would be difficult to argue against a teacher who is sensitive, flexible, creative, dynamic or graceful, compelling, vivid or bold. It reflects the idea that 'good teaching is essentially experimental, and habit, if it is permitted to encroach too far on practice, will erode curiosity and prevent the possibility of experiment' (Ruddock, J, in Moore, A, 2004, p10).

> *Artistry is important because teachers who function artistically in the classroom not only provide children with important sources of artistic experience, they also provide a climate that welcomes exploration and risk taking and encourages the disposition to play*
>
> (Eisner, 1985, p183).

Teachers like Miss Hamble, sharing Eisner's influence from art and artistry, would embrace the following ideas:

- risk;
- uncertainty;
- invention;
- creativity;
- individual and group work;
- playfulness.

From the variety of teaching approaches we have seen so far you will be aware of the increasing range of decisions a teacher has to make. This process of decision making influences the learning environment and ultimately the learning encounter for children. For example, how will you choose to organise materials? How much choice will there be? Will you include elements of skill development? Is there an opportunity for skill application? How much room is there for the development of personal ideas? Will children work on their own, in pairs or groups, and how will these be determined?

You will be able to explore these questions a little further in *Chapter 6: Considering teachers and teaching: practice*, where the practical side of teaching is approached in more detail. For now you are asked to keep thinking about what shapes the decision making process of teaching. At times the influences come from within, from our values, from tradition and the past. Increasingly they come from our experiences, the relationships and encounters which shape how we think and act. The culture in which we live and work in many ways shapes the way we think and behave.

A step towards becoming the teacher of art and design you would like to be, or indeed the primary school teacher you would like to be, is to realise that others have been there before, like Marion Richardson or Dick Field or Miss Hamble; also, we tend to work within particular traditions of education. These traditions tend not to be displayed explicitly on school walls, but they are implied in the actions and events, conversations and experiences of all schools. It is our belief that if you recognise these traditions you can a) be reflective and critical; b) move between different traditions at different times; and c) choose an alternative when appropriate.

Relating each of the teaching portraits to traditions in education

The Education for All (EFA) Global Monitoring Report (UNESCO, 2005), reported on behalf of the United Nations Educational, Scientific and Cultural Organisation (UNESCO), that to understand educational provision it is useful to look at traditions of education. In a similar way to our portraits, the 'sketches' of traditions provide useful images of teachers, and the ways in which they operate. Again, like our portraits, these sketches can help you think about yourself as a teacher, through comparison, empathy or aspiration.

Sketch A: the behaviourist tradition

As with other teaching approaches, those adopting a 'behaviourist' approach want to do what is 'right' for children. Put simply, behaviourist theory promotes a number of ideas which suggest behaviour, our thoughts and actions, can be manipulated and changed through repeated forms of reward and punishment. Schools have adopted these methods in many forms and to varying degrees, although usually to a lesser extent than those demonstrated in more extreme psychological experiments. The EFA Report (UNESCO 2005) identifies the characteristics of behaviourist theory in the classroom as including:

- standardised and externally controlled curricula;
- prescribed objectives determined independently of the learner;
- regular feedback to maintain, guide and motivate the learner;
- careful monitoring and assessment of learning, against pre-set criteria;
- teacher-directed learning, taking on the role of the expert, controlling stimuli and responses;

- incremental learning tasks to support desired cognitive development;
- use of reward and punishment allied to progress towards desired outcomes.

(UNESCO, 2005, p33)

You will be able to make connections between these ideas and the teachers described earlier, or to others you have encountered in school.

Sketch B: the humanist tradition

The humanist tradition works in ways almost opposite to the behaviourist tradition, although it still aims to promote individual wellbeing, and do 'the right thing' for children, the means to achieve the ends are very different.

Humanist traditions tend to work from a belief that children are essentially good, and as such are intrinsically motivated. They suggest that children are born unique, and operate within the relative influences of their communities, environments and cultures. The extent to which these influences are considered varies between the extremes of humanist tradition, but one of the general principles is that learners are central to making sense of their experiences of the world, and often do so within learning communities. (UNESCO identify key thinkers in this tradition as Dewey, 1916 and Vygotsky, 1978.)

The EFA Report (UNESCO, 2005) identifies the following key characteristics of humanist theory in the classroom:

- *Standardised and externally-controlled curricula are rejected.*
- *Learners construct their own meaning in flexible and responsive learning programmes.*
- *Assessment and feedback focuses on individual learning.*
- *Self-assessment and peer assessment contribute to awareness of learning.*
- *Teachers are considered as facilitators.*
- *Individual needs are recognised as operating in social networks.*

(UNESCO, 2005, p32)

Again, some of these values or ideas you will recognise. A third tradition takes a more critical approach to the situations that teachers and children find themselves in.

Sketch C: the critical tradition

On the face of it, a role for education is to transmit the values of a particular culture at a particular time. In many ways this seems fairly reasonable, as schools promote appropriate behaviour and values, and pass on concepts, knowledge and skills from the sciences, the arts and the humanities. In the process of transmission schools inadvertently repeat the things that are deemed important to a particular culture, regardless of how that culture might be changing or evolving. The transmission process is governed by particular politically-motivated policies, and in worse case scenarios leave *others* out of the process. The others face the possibility of becoming marginalised by the very thing that is intended to liberate them: education. The *others* might be defined by class, religion, gender, sexuality, age, ability or disability. Educators who adopt what is sometimes called a critical pedagogy find ways to change the social and political landscape of schools, by seeking equality and justice. (UNESCO suggest key thinkers in this tradition are Friere, 1985 and Giroux, 1993.)

The EFA Report (UNESCO, 2005) identifies the characteristics of critical theory as:

- *Education that prompts social change.*
- *Teaching which promotes critical stances to knowledge and power.*
- *Curricula that provide opportunities for questioning and change.*
- *Active participation by learners in the design of their own learning experience and environment.*

(UNESCO, 2005, p34)

It may be a little more difficult to imagine teachers or schools who share these ideals. However, there is scope here for you to think about yourself as a critical and reflective teacher who, at the very least, asks questions.

PRACTICAL TASK PRACTICAL TASK **PRACTICAL TASK** PRACTICAL TASK **PRACTICAL TASK**

Refer to Figure 5.1. Read the strategies, role of teacher and role of pupil – which of these statements best suit your ideal teacher?

Observe an art and design lesson from Teachers TV, using Figure 5.1 as a prompt sheet to analyse the programme in terms of teaching and learning. Is there a tendency for the teacher to commit to a particular teaching approach or do they move around at different times, during a lesson: for example, offering more subject-centred support and then shifting to more pupil-led support?

Learning to teach by being critical and reflective

A requirement of teacher education is to be involved in a process of review and evaluation of teaching and personal development. The Professional Standards for Qualified Teacher Status (TDA, 2007) confirm that intending teachers need to:

Reflect on and improve their practice and take responsibility for identifying and meeting their professional needs.

(Q7)

Have a creative and constructively critical approach towards innovation, being prepared to adapt their practice where benefits and improvements are identified.

(Q8)

In many institutions this is supported by a commitment to what is commonly referred to as reflective practice (Schön, 1987). In various forms this involves processes of evaluation, review, self-evaluation, reflection and criticism. In the context of teaching this can occur during school placements where you are asked to evaluate lessons, reflecting on progress made in terms of teaching and learning. This type of self-evaluation inevitably turns the focus upon yourself as the teacher, as you weigh up what teaching interventions were deemed appropriate or useful, and what aspects of teaching can be described in terms of strength or weakness. While there is an obvious worth to this sort of analysis, difficulties with the process do arise; evaluation and reflection can seem repetitive, almost 'ritualistic' with 'diminishing returns' (Moore, 2004), and an occasional sense of over-introspection.

Teaching approaches	Pupil-centred	Content-centred Student–initiated	Subject-centred
Teacher example	Portrait 1 Mrs Adams	Portrait 3 Miss Hamble	Portrait 2 Ms Evans
Orientations/ intentions	Personal growth, emotional needs, learning through art and design	Motivation to learn, in, through and about art and design	Art and design knowledge, skills and ability, learning in art and design
Strategies	Stimulating context, variety of tasks, with different foci, individual help and support	Motivating context, broad objectives, interesting tasks including exploration, project/ problem based	Structured lesson, defined objectives, clear instructions, range of resources
Role of teacher	Learning partner, giving recognition and support	Facilitator offering guidance and support	Instruction and direction
Role of pupil	Participation in learning situations – discovery and learning in all situations	Inquirer, motivated to self exploration of knowledge and interest	Learner to acquire knowledge and skills
Assessment criteria	Individual development, expression	Creativity, participation, knowledge and skill	Knowledge and skill and creativity
Outcome	Process	Process and product	Product
Education tradition	Humanist	Humanist/critical	Behaviourist

Figure 5.1 Teaching approaches and traditions, adapted from Lam (2000)

To move beyond limited notions of self-evaluation or reflection, it is useful, as described above, to see yourself in traditions of education. This approach goes some way to supporting a more *distanced* consideration of evaluating, and reflecting upon, teaching. This will help you to take stock of your development within more complex and unpredictable accounts of teaching and learning – and to do so, not in the sense of trying to overcome the problems but to acknowledge the challenges and tensions in teaching, to see how they fit with other ideas of education, through theory and practice, and to consider alternatives.

There is potential to shift around the complex ideas of teaching, taking different positions, accepting some, rejecting others, retrying earlier ones, dependent on what you are teaching, to whom, and at what time and place. In other words things change, and it is in this change that you are encouraged to see yourself differently at different times. If this means you think yourself inexperienced on one occasion you may feel more confident at another time. Inevitably this involves looking at yourself, but holds off on reducing you to a fixed type, or level, or standard, or tradition.

> **PRACTICAL TASK** PRACTICAL TASK PRACTICAL TASK PRACTICAL TASK PRACTICAL TASK
>
> Refer to a lesson and lesson plan that you have taught or helped to teach. With reference to the characteristics of educational traditions described in this chapter, review and evaluate the lesson. Think about the decision-making process you undertook and the teaching actions you made. Did they support learning which you could describe in behaviourist, humanist or critical terms?

Starting from yourself

> *All of us carry, however provisionally, a notion of what we need to be doing and achieving in order to be happy with our professional actions and our correspond-ing relationships.*

(Moore, 2004, p9)

As Moore suggests, we may well have an idea of what we should be doing when we teach; he adds that meeting the demands of those expectations is slightly more problematic. As you will be aware the demands are many. For art and design, like other subjects, you are expected to be confident with appropriate subject knowledge, and the associated skills, as well as the range of pedagogic knowledge and skills we have been describing.

The suggestions so far have asked you to listen to other people's notions of teachers and teachers of primary art and design. It is important that you keep sight of the value of looking at yourself, and what you bring to teaching and learning environments. In other words, you are not an empty vessel waiting to be filled up; you will hold beliefs and ideas, possess skills, knowledge and experience.

The purpose of this section of the chapter is to help you see yourself as a teacher of primary art and design, based on prior experiences, skills, knowledge and understanding. To help make sense of this diverse range we are suggesting a *continuum of experience, needs, confidence and support* which moves between three phases of experience:

- *Introductory level*: probably with limited experience of art and design and as result seeks support and guidance to gain confidence.
- *Threshold level*: probably with some experience in art and design and a reasonable level of confidence, works with guidance and support but is willing to try things out and offer some new suggestions.
- *Beyond threshold level*: probably secure with many areas of art and design and happy to live with some risk and uncertainty, willing to try things out within existing plans and suggest new ideas.

The following examples are typical descriptions of the continuum levels expressed here by imaginary students in the first year of a 3-year initial teacher training course.

> **PRACTICAL TASK** PRACTICAL TASK PRACTICAL TASK PRACTICAL TASK PRACTICAL TASK
>
> Read the levels described below and identify yourself somewhere on the continuum. Keep in mind that you will shift around between levels in different contexts and at different times. What would be appropriate action to take to support your professional development dependent on level? For example, it may be useful to read more widely about art and design education, or visit a gallery. It may be useful to visit a school described as having an Arts Mark award, taking time to observe some art and design lessons. You may feel your needs are best addressed by visiting and talking to an art and design subject co-ordinator to experience first hand their planning processes and teaching approaches. Alternatively a website may support and develop your awareness of assessment strategies for art and design.

Introductory level: Claire

Claire considers herself to be at an introductory level when she thinks about herself as an art and design teacher. Her experience of art and design at school was limited, and could not really be described as positive. She felt she lacked the skills and ability to draw things as they appeared. However, she remains enthusiastic about other art forms, particularly dance, which she followed as part of her post-16 education.

Claire describes the thought of teaching drawing to 10 year olds as 'slightly worrying'. When asked to list the words or phrases she associated personally with teaching art and design, including confidence, skills and knowledge, Claire included:

- slightly nervous;
- willing;
- limited knowledge of artists;
- very limited knowledge of contemporary artists;
- no drawing ability;
- enjoy taking photographs;
- enjoy dance activities.

Threshold level: David

David suggests he feels OK about trying some art and design activities in school: 'I'm looking forward to trying some things out', although the thought of 'messing up the classroom' makes him a little nervous. His own experience of the arts has been slightly narrow, but in terms of art and design fairly positive. He gained a B at GCSE art and considered the option of AS level Photography or Graphics, resisting the choice on the advice of his family, in his preparation to be a primary school teacher. David speaks enthusiastically about his GCSE art and design teacher, and is full of admiration for their sense of adventure, combined with rigour and discipline. When asked to list the words or phrases he associated personally with teaching art and design, including confidence, skills and knowledge, David included:

- interested;
- fairly confident (with some aspects);
- uncertain about work with clay;
- willing;
- excited about working with photography;
- some knowledge of artists from twentieth century;
- limited awareness of sculptors or craftspeople.

Post-threshold level: Emma

Emma studied art and design at GCSE and continued her studies to A level gaining a grade B. Her course was predominantly drawing and painting, but encouraged a creative approach to materials and ideas, documenting the learning process in a sketchbook. She says, 'I love art, it's a great chance for me to express myself and my ideas...I can't wait to teach art in school.' Emma talks enthusiastically about the potential of drawing, not only for explaining things but for imagining new things. This she says is 'down to her art teacher at school, she was always going on about the power of drawing'. Emma adds that she is looking forward to the special subject art and design element of the course, where she hopes to find out more about the whole business of art and design education. When asked to list the words or phrases she associated personally with teaching art and design, including confidence, skills and knowledge, Emma included:

- willing;
- excited;
- confident with most areas of practical activity;
- a little unsure about using video or ICT;
- some confidence with artists and designers;
- not sure about craftspeople;
- keen to find out more!

These phases will be referred to directly and indirectly in the remaining chapters, and throughout the book, as you consider what you need to know, what skills you may need to develop or what you need to do to plan, prepare or teach art and design. At times the planning, teaching and assessment will meet your needs at an introductory level; at other times you may feel more confident and want to take some risks with elements of the lesson; at other times you may want to venture into the type of teaching which follows a humanist tradition, applying its principles to planning, resourcing and assessment.

REFLECTIVE TASK

This reflective task asks you to take stock of the thoughts you have about being a teacher. It involves making lists of words, which can be used to help you reflect and evaluate your current teaching position and possible alternatives.

Make a list of the 15 verbs which describe what teachers do: e.g. challenge, demonstrate, encourage, structure, support, transform, value.

Make a list of 10 adverbs which describe the ways in which teachers do these things: e.g. carefully, creatively, clearly, sensitively, imaginatively, intelligently, willingly.

Think about the traditions of teaching. How do your verbs and adverbs tie in with the different types of teacher and teaching approach? Do you find yourself drawn to particular verbs and adverbs which describe 'you' as a teacher?

Becoming a teacher is a long process; it starts well before an initial teacher training programme and ends well beyond the graduating ceremony. As you move towards becoming the teacher you want to be you will see and hear echoes of your teacher reflected in the actions and words of others. Eventually you will be able to accommodate similar actions and words, and craft them to your own teacher identity. This chapter has introduced some options and variations of art and design teachers, from whom you can pick and choose, shape and change.

Chapter 6: Considering teachers and teaching: practice will develop the practical role of the teacher of primary art and design, offering a range of approaches to teaching, including strategies for initiating ideas, supporting and developing ideas through shared language (productive metaphors), organising the classroom, and using resources.

A SUMMARY OF **KEY POINTS**

> Teachers adopt different approaches to teaching.

> Approaches are shaped by tradition and changing ideas about art and design education.

> Different approaches result in different relationships with children and their ideas.

> Your approach will be shaped by your experiences, the teachers you meet and the values you hold.

> Your approach and teacher identity will change and vary, drawing on different traditions, at different times.

MOVING *ON* > > > > > > MOVING *ON* > > > > > > MOVING *ON*

Welcome the opportunity to see yourself within a long line of teachers who shift and move, as they review their ideas about children, about learning, about schooling and about art and design.

REFERENCES REFERENCES **REFERENCES** REFERENCES **REFERENCES** REFERENCES

Barnes, R (2006) *Teaching art to young children 4–9*, 2nd edn. Abingdon: RoutledgeFalmer.

DfEE (1999) *The National Curriculum*. London: HMSO.

Dewey, J (1916) *Democracy and Education*. New York: Macmillan.

Eisner, EW (1985) *The educational imagination*: *On the design and evaluation of school programs*. London: Macmillan.

Eisner, EW (2003) Artistry in education. *Scandinavian Journal of Educational Research*, 47(3): 373–84.

Field, D (1973) Art and art education, in Field, D and Newick, J *The study of education and art*. London: Routledge and Kegan Paul.

Freire, P (1985) *The politics of education: Culture, power and liberation. London: Macmillan.*

Goroux, H (1993) Living dangerously. New York: Peter Lang.

Hallam, J, Lee, H and das Gupta, M (2002) An Analysis of the Presentation of Art in the British Primary School Curriculum and its Implications for Teaching. *Journal of Art and Design Education*, 26(2) 2007, pp206–214.

Lam, BH (2008) Secondary Art School Teachers' Concepts of Teaching in Hong Kong. *International Journal of Art and Design Education*, 19(2) 2008, pp208–216.

Moore, A (2004) *The good teacher: dominant discourses in teaching and teacher education.* Abingdon: RoutledgeFalmer.

Richardson, M (1948) *Art and the child.* London: University of London Press.

Schön, D (1987) *Educating the reflective practitioner.* San Francisco, CA: Jossey-Bass.

TDA (2008) *Professional Standards for Qualified Teacher Status and Requirements for Initial Teacher Training (revised 2008)* available at http://www.tda.gov.uk/partners/ittstandardfs.aspx accessed July 2009.

UNESCO (2005) Education for All global monitoring report, *Understanding Education Quality* available at: portal.unesco.org/education/en/ev.php-URL_ID=35939&URL_DO=DO_TOPIC&URL_SECTION=201.html (accessed 02/05/09).

Vygotsky, LS (1978) *Mind in Society: The development of higher pyschological processes*. Cambridge MA: Harvard University Press.

Wilson, B (1992) Primitivism, the avant-garde and the art of little children, in Thistlewood, D (ed) *Drawing research and development*. Harlow: Longman.

FURTHER READING FURTHER READING **FURTHER READING** FURTHER READING

Atkinson, D (2002) *Art in education: Identity and practice*. London: Kluwer.

Macdonald, S (2004) *The history and philosophy of art education*. Cambridge: Lutterworth Press. The Recognition of Child Art, pp. 320–354.

6
Considering teachers and teaching: practice

Chapter objectives

By the end of this chapter you will have:

- **developed an awareness of yourself as a potential teacher of art and design;**
- **developed an awareness of the decision-making process of teaching;**
- **increased your awareness of strategies to support and challenge learning in art and design.**

This chapter addresses the following Standards for QTS: **Q1, Q10, Q14, Q15, Q25.**

Key themes: teacher interventions; support and challenge; intervention and observation; professional understanding; decision making; choice taking.

Introduction

During the everyday encounters of a primary classroom, teachers face choices and make decisions. A responsibility for any teacher is to make considered decisions in the range of situations in which they find themselves. For the teacher of art and design this is no different. The considered decisions should be made to 'help children towards imaginative and purposeful responses in art and design'.

For example, choices will include:

- which materials to provide and which to leave in the cupboard;
- whether to demonstrate a technique or not;
- whether to show someone how to use shading to depict a human nose;
- how long to continue an activity before the noise level is deemed unacceptable;
- what to say when a 4-year-old shows you their drawing and says nothing;
- what to say to a 7-year-old when they say they 'can't draw dogs';
- which artists to include and which to leave out;
- how to respond to negative comments about a chosen artist's work.

The list goes on. Making decisions and responding to scenarios like those listed above can be challenging, and in many ways experience is the thing which helps in the decision-making process. When you observe experienced teachers you will notice they make decisions almost intuitively.

To help you make sense of the range of choices and associated decisions, we can refer to categories offered by Eisner (2002). He describes these categories as 'forces which influence learning' (Eisner, 2002, p71):

1. materials and activities: which offer potential or limitation;
2. prompts, cues and scaffolding from teachers: which provide challenge and support;
3. classroom norms: which establish expectations and boundaries;
4. classroom ambience: which encourages attitudes and making allowances.

(Eisner, 2002, p71)

In the teaching situations you find yourself in, you will be able to anticipate some of the choices and decisions by thinking ahead within these categories. This will help you develop a repertoire of appropriate responses to help children towards imaginative and purposeful responses in art and design. You will be able to think about materials, about the type of support and challenge you will offer, and about the purposeful atmosphere you wish to encourage. As we have suggested elsewhere, the development of this repertoire will be supported by your committed and reflective approach to teaching and learning.

REFLECTIVE TASK

From your experiences as a student, think about your observations of lessons in primary schools. Can you remember times when a teacher has appeared to make decisions effortlessly and almost intuitively, as they move between ideas and pupils, with a sense of purpose and confidence? Think about how the activities, resources and materials have helped teachers work in a confident way, helping them to be organised, with a sense of purpose and direction. Consider how children have responded to the activities and the materials. Have they been eager and excited?

Figure 6.1 Supporting children's learning in art and design with demonstrations and examples, and by matching materials to challenges

Helping children towards imaginative and purposeful responses in art and design

Materials and activities

The materials offered to children, allied to related activities, almost inevitably offer possibilities and limitations. If materials are given to children, or made available, children will be able to conjure up ideas from the materials, combine them in unusual and imaginative ways, or develop ways of applying previously acquired skills to the materials. Providing an extensive range of materials may appear the obvious way to open up creative and artistic responses, however this is not always the case. For some artists, working with a very limited range of materials forces them to act in more imaginative and purposeful ways. For example, musicians will compose music around limited and repetitive phrases; visual artists will limit their palette to certain colours, or produce imaginary drawn landscapes using nothing more than graphite and an eraser. Sculptors will manipulate and construct with a single material, for example steel, for their entire artistic adult life.

CASE STUDY 6.1a

The children working with Mrs Adams were presented with an extensive range of materials while those working with Ms Evans had fewer choices from a limited range.

The extensive range gives the sense of freedom and choice, a sense of adventure and creativity; the more limited range appears slightly restrictive, less ambitious and less creative. However, the teachers were establishing different intentions for their lessons: for Ms Evans the choice of materials was limited to encourage a focused and sustained approach to colour and composition, developing particular skills and knowledge.

Activities which promote learning in art and design need to maintain a sense of purpose, and where possible a sense of ambition. When making decisions about the sort of activity you want children to be engaged in, ask yourself:

- Is the activity active?
- Is it challenging for this age group?
- Is it interesting?
- Is the activity short enough or long enough?
- Is there variety during the activity?
- How will you punctuate the activity with new challenge or support?
- Will the results be varied and interesting?
- Will the children talk positively about the experience?
- Would a change of scale add to the activity, either very small or very large?
- Does the activity build on, extend or enrich previous activity?
- Would working in groups or pairs add to the activity?
- Is there room for personal ideas to develop?
- Is there space for skills and knowledge to be acquired, developed and applied?
- Do the materials provided support the activity intended?

PRACTICAL TASK PRACTICAL TASK **PRACTICAL TASK** PRACTICAL TASK **PRACTICAL TASK**

Review an art and design lesson you have been involved with, as the teacher or learner. Where possible look back at the planning and think about what happened during the lesson. Against the bullet points above provide a checklist of the suitability of materials and activities to help children towards imaginative and purposeful responses in art and design.

Challenge and support, prompts, cues and scaffolding

In schools the level of support offered to children during art and design remains varied. There are teachers who support and foster an environment which is led by children's ideas, and there are those who teach with more direct intervention. The debate about which is 'correct' remains long standing:

> *To teach or not; to intervene, to direct, to instruct, to demonstrate or not. This dilemma is to be found no more acutely than in art education where there are perennial arguments about such topics as whether to demonstrate or not; whether to teach technique; whether to use the blackboard or work on a child's picture.*
>
> (Gentle, 1986, Introduction)

CASE STUDY 6.1b

Mrs Adams's support and intervention is through the encouragement of personal ideas and creative outcomes; she welcomes these and provides materials to support their generation. Ms Evans is more direct in her approach. She provides resources to direct her teaching around, she focuses children with the use of learning outcomes, and she uses an interactive whiteboard to demonstrate colour mixing.

These different approaches offer different support and challenge to children and encourage different responses. It is possible to support creative outcomes with direct intervention, or more discrete intervention, employed in a supportive and encouraging environment.

Burton (2001) observed that teacher interventions, scaffolding, cues and prompts, can support learning during lessons, as shown in Figure 6.2.

Although the list in Figure 6.2 is not exhaustive, you will be able to identify some of the strategies from your experiences of primary classrooms to support and challenge children. There is an indication in Figure 6.2 that lessons are divided into a series of parts, but you will also be increasingly aware, through your reflective and considered approach to teaching, that the parts can be interchanged, repeated or rotated to adapt and change to the learning environment, and to the needs of children.

PRACTICAL TASK PRACTICAL TASK **PRACTICAL TASK** PRACTICAL TASK **PRACTICAL TASK**

Visit Teachers TV on the internet and navigate your way to the primary art and design video resources. Select a video resource and watch the video. Note down the following headings on a sheet of paper:

- opening strategies;
- organisational strategies;
- instructional strategies;
- motivational strategies;
- questioning strategies;
- closing strategies.

Against each heading make notes to describe the teacher's interventions, and their strategies for support and challenge.

Opening strategies
Listening to a story
Looking at postcards
Watching a film
Going for a walk
Taking a series of photographs
Exploring materials for 3 minutes
Setting and responding to a challenge
Handling objects
Listening to music

Organisational strategies
Direct presentation
Group discussion
Individual work
Small group work
Whole-class collaborations
One-to-one work with pupils
Demonstration
Exploration of materials
Use of ICT for instruction
Review of work

Instructional strategies
Providing step-by-step demonstration
Offering a pupil demonstration
Showing a finished example
Showing a progressive series of examples
Encouraging free exploration
Guiding pupil practice

Motivational strategies
Setting challenges
Establishing time frames
Introducing new ideas during lessons
Offering positive and specific feedback
Including work in display or presentation

Questioning strategies
Asking closed questions
Asking open-ended questions
Encouraging group discussion
Facilitating mind mapping
Talking to children in a one-to-one conversation
Checking for understanding through prompts and questions

Closing strategies
Emphasising key ideas
Reflecting on the activity
Summarising the activity
Relating ideas to the activity
Reinforcing and praising responses
Showing personal satisfaction

after Burton (2001)

Figure 6.2 Art and design teacher interventions

Classroom norms, establishing expectations and boundaries

Teachers form relationships with children in classrooms, along corridors and on the play-ground. The relationships are articulated and expressed through conversations, through the actions and decisions we take in response to children's needs, and children's reactions to teacher interventions. It is during these relationships and encounters with children, that teachers share their expectations and establish boundaries.

During lessons, teachers establish their expectations by encouraging children to negotiate the boundaries; it may be that the more interesting and creative work takes place when the boundaries are negotiated together; where the boundaries are gently pushed and nudged a little.

CASE STUDY 6.1c

Mrs Adams begins a lesson by sitting on the floor. She gathers children round her and shares ideas with them. She encourages children to produce their own imagery, with apparently very few boundaries and expectations of pupils, other than enjoying the opportunity to emotionally express themselves.

Ms Evans appears to have established more specific boundaries, in the choice of materials, the subject matter for the children's imagery, the organisation of resources, the use of the interactive whiteboard and by establishing and sharing learning intentions.

When engaged in teaching art and design you may find yourself torn between a number of opposing aims and intentions, which inevitably balance between a variety of boundaries and expectations. The balance between freedom and control is perhaps the most often cited example. If you establish a situation in a classroom which encourages a certain element of freedom for children, a shift in the control boundary will be necessary. You may feel slightly uncomfortable with this scenario as an intending teacher, or even an experienced one, particularly as the materials in art and design lessons are potentially 'messy'. If you are concerned, then it will be wise to exert enough control so as to maintain a grasp of the situation, but not with such a stranglehold that all imaginative response is stifled.

By doing so you will begin to pay attention to the final influence on teaching: classroom ambience or atmosphere, and how it encourages or discourages certain behaviour, includ-ing imaginative and purposeful art and design.

Classroom ambience, encouraging attitudes and making allowances

Some teachers of art and design actively encourage a more relaxed and informal approach to lessons. They may share ideas in more open and negotiated ways, listening to pupil ideas and taking on board their suggestions; they encourage personal ideas to be developed and explored. Learning is open ended and initiated in many ways by pupils themselves, actively engaged in purposeful making. Children are encouraged to select resources, make choices and evaluate their progress; above all they are encouraged to act as artists (Eisner, 2002).

You can ask:

- Do I trust pupils with materials?
- If not, what can I do to establish an environment of trust?
- Are ideas presented in interesting and varied ways?
- Is there a sense of ambition and purpose to the activities and lessons?
- Is there flexibility in the planning and resourcing of lessons?
- Are pupils motivated by the intrinsic nature of their artistic explorations?

CASE STUDY 6.2

Miss Hamble developed an art week based around the initial sketchbook explorations of her pupils. She initiated the activities based on pupil interest and set challenges to the group with a sense of purpose and ambition. The learning intentions remained open and to a degree were flexible, although there was some emphasis given to learning through art: to co-operate, share ideas, and listen to others. There was a real sense of the children being encouraged to work as artists.

REFLECTIVE TASK

Make a list of words which best describe the atmosphere you wish to generate to support learning in art and design lessons. Consider the list and think about any barriers which may get in the way of such aspirations.

Ask yourself if you trust children, with materials and ideas. If not, consider ways to be more positive about the work they may achieve and the ideas they could have. If you are thinking the children you have worked with need closer attention and smaller steps towards choice and trust, think about how you could make those small steps, without leaving yourself feeling vulnerable or setting children completely adrift.

One of the great things about teaching art and design, as mentioned earlier, is the lack of restraint from any national strategy; there is no national primary strategy for art and design, thank goodness. However, while this may present opportunities for some, for others it presents challenges. This will be dependent on how positive you may be feeling towards teaching in general and to the subject of art and design. With little obvious guidance, teachers turn to other teaching strategies and initiatives and transfer them to art and design; they may turn to other colleagues (perhaps the art and design subject leader) or they may look in the National Curriculum or the QCA schemes of work. In both these documents there is limited guidance to support actual teaching, although both encourage active intervention and teaching with the phrase *'pupils should be taught'*.

Teaching and the National Curriculum for art and design

The following interventions are structured around the processes indicated in the National Curriculum (DfEE, 1999) and in the supporting areas of knowledge and understanding.

Helping children explore and develop ideas

- Provide stimulating resources: objects, experiences, events.
- Show children video or film clips.
- Take children for walks.
- Take photographs.
- Collect objects, cuttings, memories.
- Record feelings, observations, smells, in words or pictures.
- Shoot video footage.
- Tell stories.
- Read poems.
- Observe with viewfinders.
- Help children to visualise or imagine.
- Visualise and imagine alongside children.

Helping children investigate and make

- Demonstrate techniques.
- Encourage children to use sketchbooks to try things out.
- Show examples of artists' sketchbooks.
- Investigate work in your own sketchbook.
- Explore material properties with children.
- Challenge children to select and combine materials.
- Guide children towards selecting or combining materials.
- Do not get too hung up when things do not work out.
- Suggest alternatives.
- Question children about their choices.
- Value children's responses.
- Provide examples of material use or techniques by other artists, craftspeople or designers.
- Discuss the range of responses in the class.
- Organise materials for accessibility.

Helping children review and develop ideas

- Listen carefully to responses.
- Provide vocabulary charts to support responses.
- Share ideas with others.
- Suggest criteria for evaluating work.
- Record observations of artists' work.
- List words connected to artists' work.
- Suggest alternatives.
- Encourage children to try things out.
- Try some experiments alongside children.
- Suggest a change in scale.
- Photocopy work.
- Scan work and project it via the data projector.
- Make notes alongside the projected image.
- Encourage experiments on copies of work.
- Record and document processes of working with photographs and words.
- Encourage children to document and review own process of working with words and photographs.

Helping children understand the visual tactile and spatial qualities of art and design

- Provide examples of visual, tactile and spatial qualities in made and found worlds.
- Provide examples of visual, tactile and spatial qualities in the work of artists, craftspeople and designers.
- Produce a list of appropriate vocabulary.
- Talk about visual, tactile and spatial qualities.
- Develop and extend vocabulary.
- Notice the visual, tactile and spatial qualities in ordinary things.

Helping children understand the work of others

- Have an artist of the month.
- Visit a gallery; visit a gallery online.
- Make connections between artists' work.
- Identify similarities and differences in artists' work.
- Extend the range of artists, craftspeople and designers.
- Use themes to connect artists, craftspeople and designers.
- Display examples of architects, graphic designers, product designers, jewellery makers, photographers, ceramicists, printmakers.

Making decisions

It is likely that your early teaching experiences will be supported by the planning, teaching, and assessment strategies of the classroom teacher with whom you find yourself working. This supportive environment will make positive contributions to your development, as you ebb and flow between what we are describing as the introductory, threshold and post-threshold levels of a beginning teacher.

REFLECTIVE TASK

Look at and consider Figure 6.4 Making decisions, on page 102. Do you consider yourself, on the whole, an introductory, threshold or post-threshold teacher? (Remember that your position could change dependent on what you will be teaching; for example, you may be more confident handling colour and paint than teaching drawing.) Think about the decisions you will make to support a safe and purposeful working environment. Do not worry if you cannot achieve everything at once, but set yourself goals to work towards under the four headings: materials and activities; cues, prompts and scaffolding; classroom norms; and classroom atmosphere.

As you gain experience of primary education and primary schooling, your teaching expertise will develop to a point where the decision-making process is initiated more by you. In other words, you will be in a proactive position to ask questions regarding the nature of your teaching and what is being taught. You will be able to consider the development of children's work beyond the lesson. In this way lessons can be seen as developmental learning experiences. Your approach to assessment and evaluation will be more sophisticated, and probably at this point you will be asking questions regarding creative art and design lessons.

Your teaching approach will develop a more refined vocabulary, which helps you articulate ideas clearly and with purpose. This refinement comes from what Prentice (1998) refers to as *professional understanding*. This position allows you to integrate your subject knowledge

---

Colour

Key terms
- Primary colour: colour that cannot be obtained by mixing.
- Secondary colour: made from mixtures of two primaries.
- Tertiary colour: a mix of one primary and one secondary, effectively three colours.
- Complementary colours: colours which react most with each other and are opposite on the colour wheel.
- Discords: secondary-to-secondary pairings of colours.
- Tone: lightness and darkness of colour.
- Hue: the property of a colour that enables it to be identified as red, yellow, etc.
- Intensity: saturation, the brightness or brilliance of a colour.
- Intensity: chroma, the purity of a colour.
- Monochrome: single colour scheme.
- Achromatic: black and white.

Qualities of colour
cold, warm, bold, hot, temperate, natural, industrial, saturated, bright, intense, subtle, deep, delicate, strong, fierce, quiet, loud, limited-range, broad-range contrast harmony block-colour, colour-field, opaque, transparent, translucent, iridescent, fluorescent.

Application of colour
over-lay, under-paint, thick, impasto, thin, washes, scratch, dry-brush.

Figure 6.3 Using vocabulary to help children develop their understanding of visual, tactile and spatial qualities

with increasing pedagogical knowledge. You will be able to transform ideas and share them eloquently with children, via explanations, instructions, stories, analogies, metaphors and questions (Prentice, 1998).

In art and design the vocabulary illustrated in Figure 6.3 (and developed for other visual elements in *Chapter 4: Knowledge and understanding: progression of experiences and processes*) will help you talk about a particular area of the curriculum with confidence. In the example given, your subject knowledge can be demonstrated in your expression of ideas regarding colour, exploring and developing children's knowledge and understanding:

- Challenge pupils to mix secondary colours with primary colours.
- Challenge pupils to apply colour in three distinct ways.
- Challenge pupils to show depth in colour by over-painting.
- Ask pupils to identify from a selection a painting with passages of bold colour or areas of quiet, subtle colour.
- Ask pupils to name colours according to their quality: fiery red, syrupy yellow.
- Challenge pupils to combine coloured materials to show texture.
- Challenge pupils to combine coloured materials from the same colour palette.

A challenge for all teachers is how to move children's ideas forward, how to help develop their ideas or initial responses. To foster development demands an awareness of what might be possible with particular age groups. *Chapter 8: Assessment, monitoring and feedback*

	Introductory	Threshold	Post-threshold
Materials and activities	Encourage safe use of materials. Offer some choice. Prepare carefully alongside teacher. Provide sufficient materials. Match materials to the activity. Develop activity appropriate for age group.	Encourage safe use of materials. Offer some choice. Prepare and plan activities which develop ideas. Change materials to add challenge. Extend responses with additional activities.	Encourage safe use of materials. Offer choice where appropriate. Think of unusual materials. Develop activities from children's ideas. Guide children towards choosing materials to match ideas.
Support and challenge, cues, prompts and scaffolding	Work alongside class teacher. Support a group. Give clear instructions. Demonstrate skills carefully. Use prepared examples. Close lessons with reviews of work.	Teach independently. Offer clear instructions. Demonstrate skills. Review work as lessons progress. Interrupt lessons at relevant points. Set clear challenges. Close lessons with reviews of work.	Begin lessons in imaginative ways. Challenge pupils with long and short activities. Review individual progress and offer feedback. Share criteria for assessment. Close lessons with self evaluations. Close lessons with new challenges.
Classroom norms	Have high expectations. Be careful not to underestimate abilities.	Have high expectations. Marry activities with abilities. Consider individual needs.	Expect imaginative and purposeful responses. Encourage creative responses. Develop individual support.
Classroom atmosphere	Have a sense of purpose. Offer praise which is positive and specific. Encourage children to sustain effort and develop work.	Have a sense of purpose. Encourage personal work. Offer praise which is positive and specific. Challenge children.	Maintain a sense of purpose. Praise imaginative, creative and individual responses. Expect the unexpected.

Figure 6.4 Making decisions

explores this idea further. In addition you will need a willingness to explore the unknown with children, to develop more creative and imaginative responses. Again vocabulary plays an important role in your teaching approach, allowing you to question, stimulate and prompt children into further enquiry.

Figure 6.5 (on page 104) illustrates a collection of *process words* which will help you to develop creative responses with children. We have referred to the words collectively as the *Productive Toolbox*.

A note on the Productive Toolbox

The Productive Toolbox was developed and adapted from Waters (1994), as part of the Higher Education, the Arts and Schools (HEARTS) project. Established in 2003, with co-funders including the Esmée Fairbairn Foundation and the Paul Hamlyn Foundation, the HEARTS project aims to extend and develop the role of the arts in primary initial teacher education and training. The project has been extended to include eleven higher education institutions. During the HEARTS project at the University of Winchester, we introduced students to the idea of using language, described later as the 'productive toolbox', as a trigger to develop practical work. Initially the practical work had a multidisciplinary feel involving visual art, music/sound and dance/movement, and the lexicon suggested a powerful way to enquire across these disciplines. For example, where students were encouraged to accumulate, sequence, or mirror imagery in the visual arts, they could apply the same language to sound or movement.

In the review of arts practice, surveyed from a range of higher education institutions and courses, *Living without boundaries: challenging conventional artform constraints within education*, Waters (1994) presents a 'toolbox of productive metaphors' to identify common or shared artistic practices and describes them as 'compositional strategies for working across media' (Waters, 1994, p75). The metaphors are offered as an evolving and emerging lexicon. Waters adds to this, and sees the power of the metaphors working outside arts disciplines, as well as across and between them, suggesting they are *dynamic forces* 'which ideally empower the student to devise or imagine responses to any situation, irrespective of their specific skill training' (Waters, 1994, p75).

Where we have adopted the Productive Toolbox children have responded positively, using words and language to help to devise and imagine new ideas, in a range of materials and with a range of subject matter.

PRACTICAL TASK PRACTICAL TASK **PRACTICAL TASK** PRACTICAL TASK **PRACTICAL TASK**

Look at Figure 6.5 (page 104) Helping children develop creative responses in art and design. Get yourself a sketchbook – you could buy one, make one or adapt one from something else. Make an agreement with yourself that you will commit things to the sketchbook for the next month: collect photographs; make montage imagery; collect words and letters from magazines; construct Haikus; draw pictures; doodle and embellish; collect colours. As you accumulate material look through the toolbox words and apply them to develop ideas: make a collection; develop a sequence of photographs of making a cup of tea; layer and combine images to create something new; uncover areas to reveal hidden things. Begin to act like a creative artist.

The QCA (2004) suggests indicators of children being involved in creative activity involve them:

questioning and challenging
...children ask questions of materials and ideas: 'What if I combine oil pastels with ink...?' This is how I usually use paint, what happens if I try it this way?';

making connections and seeing relationships
...between children's work and artists', between materials and their intentions, between ideas in other subjects, between past and current ideas, between each other;

envisaging what might be
...imagining and visualising, in children's minds...on paper, in clay, with paint, in sketchbooks;

exploring ideas, keeping options open
...using the **toolbox of productive** words to play around and invent.

When artists play with ideas and materials they tend to work through some of these productive processes, which combine to make the Productive Toolbox:

Order	Embellish
Mask	Rotate
Layer	Mirror
Zoom	Canon
Magnify	Edit
Repeat	Filter
Loop	Extract
Accumulate	Select
Mark	Sort
Recur	Sequence
Uncover	Categorise
Excavate	Group
Accent	Collect
Dissect	Arrange
Scale	Cover
Combine	Wrap
Juxtapose	Expand
Diffuse	Erase
Map	

Helping children play around with ideas and materials using the Productive Toolbox:

- Produce a sequence of images of your drawings, photocopied and coloured with different combinations.
- Layer materials to produce qualities of texture and surface.
- Cover parts of drawings with paper and mask areas as you apply coloured materials.
- Magnify an area of a painting with the aid of an overhead projector.
- Change the scale of your work, reduce and enlarge on the photocopier.
- Use a data projector to project words and images onto the outside of the building.
- Map routes made around the classroom in one day.
- Do the same for a week.
- Draw the movements of a football player during a game on TV, without looking at the drawing as you trace their movements.
- Embellish and decorate work using the colour schemes of particular artists.
- Select a series of images and present them in a sequence to show your lunchtime experience.
- Document the lunchtime experience as a fold-out book.
- Sort your favourite toys by size, colour, texture, fabric, colour.
- Photograph each category.
- Cover your page in graphite, rub out sections with an eraser to make an image.
- Collect flotsam and jetsam and arrange as a colour wheel.
- Wrap objects in brown paper.
- Wrap the school in a roll of paper.
- Map the horizon on the paper.
- Take photographs looking down and up at points around the school.
- Combine the photographs as though they were mirror images.
- Zoom in on locations around the school.

(adapted from Waters, 1994)

Figure 6.5. Helping children develop creative responses in art and design: the productive toolbox

Learning in art and design

Processes
- explore
- develop
- investigate
- make
- evaluate

Knowledge
- materials
- visual qualities
- artists, craftspeople and designers

Skills
- production
- perception
- discussion

Values
- confidence
- willingness
- openness
- sensitivity

Learning through art and design
- Cross-curricular development
- personal development
- materials and activities
- prompts, cues and scaffolding
- classroom norms
- classroom ambience

(Eisner, 2002)

Mysterious shadows

There is a sense of excitement and intrigue as the children come back into the classroom following the lunchtime break. The room is dark and lit predominantly by candles and low-wattage spotlights. Everyday kitchen and household objects are suspended within the flickering light, casting mysterious shadows across very large pieces of crisp white paper. The children are manoeuvred gently across the beams of light, their shadows cast against the walls. Unusually for an art lesson the teacher has asked the children to remain silent in this strangely-lit classroom atmosphere. The Year 4 children can barely contain themselves. 'You'll remember over the past few weeks we've been talking about light in science and religious studies, and learning about some of its properties, qualities and significance...Who can remember what we did in art last week.... which was connected to our theme of light?' Two or three hands go up. 'Did we do some drawings with light bits and dark bits...with those messy chalk things?'

The lesson moves quickly to the shadows, and referring back to the previous sessions on light and tone the children are given a choice of charcoal or graphite pencils to produce their own 'shadow drawings'. The teacher demonstrates how to vary pressure and type of mark to control the quality and range of tone, recapping on skills from the previous week.

Working alongside a classroom assistant, two parent helpers, a student teacher and the teacher, the groups are organised at tables and make tentative beginnings to capture the qualities of the shadows. Approaches to the drawings are reserved. The teacher stops the class, gathers them together, and turns on the data projector. The intensity of its light is exaggerated in the darkened room. A collection of images is shown, some taken by the teacher of shadows around her home, of reflected light on walls, and images from the work of artists exploring light and shadows: van Gogh's *Potato Eaters* and Cornellia Parker's *30 Pieces of Silver*. 'They look like silver wheels, silver coins...is that their shadow on the floor?...Look at that, Miss, those shadows are massive.'

Just before the children return to their work, she highlights some features of the drawings so far, holding up examples of 'good use of tonal range...good use of marks to create tone...and a lovely sense of the mysterious shadows'.

Teaching art and design

Helping children explore and develop ideas:
- stimulate
- resource
- encourage
- question
- show

Helping children investigate and make:
- demonstrate
- show
- question
- provide
- investigate
- explore
- challenge
- value
- discuss

Helping children review and develop ideas:
listen
share
record
observe
suggest

Helping children understand the visual, tactile and spatial qualities of art and design:
- provide
- develop
- notice
- discuss

Helping children understand the work of others:
- show
- identify
- connect
- extend

Figure 6.6 A learning encounter on the theme of 'mysterious shadows'

REFLECTIVE TASK

As you review this chapter and the previous chapters on teaching and learning in art and design, refer to Figure 6.6, and read the ambitious learning encounter described as 'mysterious shadows'. Using the information provided in the boxes, review the lesson and the activity in terms of teaching and learning as you now understand it, in relation to primary art and design.

- What do children learn in art and design?
- What do children learn through art and design?
- How does the teacher help children to learn?
- How do materials and activities support learning?
- How do prompts and cues support learning?
- How does feedback contribute to learning?
- How would you describe the classroom atmosphere?

You will be able to recognise from the range of strategies discussed in this chapter those with which you are familiar, those which you have observed and possibly some new ideas. Making learning interesting relies on many of the ideas presented in this chapter; it involves you actively choosing to make interventions to support and develop knowledge and understanding. In many ways steps towards this situation are initiated as you plan and prepare lessons by asking relatively simple questions: How can I support children's development? What can I do to help this class understand? What can I do to motivate this group? How can I encourage this person to explore more freely?

Chapter 7 supports your development further by exploring and examining approaches to planning, an important step to formalising creative and thoughtful thinking about teaching and learning.

A SUMMARY OF KEY POINTS

> Teachers help children towards imaginative and purposeful art and design.

> Teachers motivate, develop, support and challenge.

> Teachers make decisions which provide opportunities.

> Language helps teachers respond to children's needs.

MOVING *ON* > > > > > > MOVING *ON* > > > > > > MOVING *ON*

Take the idea of the teacher into the classroom and make decisions which support and challenge. Think about your role and talk to your peers about how it compares to teaching other subjects.

REFERENCES REFERENCES **REFERENCES** REFERENCES **REFERENCES** REFERENCES

Burton, D (2001) How do we teach? Results of a national survey of instruction in Secondary Art Education. *Studies in Art Education: A journal of issues and research*, 42(2): 131–45.

DfEE (1999) *The National Curriculum*. London: HMSO.

Eisner, EW (2002) *The arts and the creation of mind*. New Haven, CT: Yale University Press.

Gentle, K (1986) *Children and art teaching*. Beckenham: Croom Helm.

Prentice, R (1998) (ed) *Teaching art and design: Addressing issues and identifying directions*. London: Cassell.

QCA (2004) *Creativity: find it, promote it*. Sudbury: QCA Publications.

Waters, S (1994) *Living without boundaries*. Bath: Bath College of Higher Education Press.

7
Planning and preparing to teach: ideas into practice

Chapter objectives

By the end of this chapter you will have:

- an understanding of the planning process in art and design, including long-term, medium-term and short-term planning;
- an understanding of how art and design principles and pedagogy explored in previous chapters of this book feed into the planning process;
- an understanding of how the experiences and processes in art and design are explored and developed through planning;
- an understanding of the importance of continuity, progression, and development when planning and preparing to teach.

This chapter addresses the following Standards for QTS: **Q3**, **Q14**, **Q15**, **Q22**.

Key themes: continuity; progression; development; experiences; processes; schemes of work; long-term, medium-term and short-term planning; objectives; lesson structure and content; evaluation and review.

Introduction

This chapter provides the opportunity to explore and understand approaches to, and stages of, the planning process for art and design in the primary school.

Planning documentation for schools in art and design is varied. Although schools acknowledge and work to national frameworks (National Curriculum, (DfEE, 1999); Early Years Foundation Stage (DCSF, 2008) the appearance and content of planning remains in the control of individual schools.

This varied picture presents something of a challenge when making sense of school planning arrangements and documentation. However, you can be confident that, while the outcomes and approaches to planning vary, all primary schools have a responsibility to organise the provision for art and design into a coherent programme. This establishes experiences which meet the requirements of the national frameworks demonstrating breadth, balance, progression, continuity and creativity. Beyond this, schools can respond to their own longer-term agenda, school ethos and staff expertise. They can document planning to include themes, experiences and processes that are relevant to their pupils' learning needs.

The organisation and focus of planning, for teaching and learning in art and design, will reflect a school's overall approach to the curriculum. For some schools this may involve a theme-based approach, for others a subject-based approach; others will plan activity weeks dedicated to the arts, or explore the arts through outdoor learning; other schools will involve and support pupil ideas in the planning process.

Despite these differences, a project or scheme of work for art and design, whether discrete, cross-curricular, term-based or during an art week, will be planned around a progressive sequence of developmental activities. This enables experiences, processes and skills to be taught, while incorporating time for exploration, development, investigation, review and evaluation.

In addition to the national frameworks, the QCA (2000) scheme of work for art and design may also shape a school's art and design planning. As these are non-statutory guidelines, the material is used at a school's discretion. Some schools choose to follow the guidelines closely while others move in alternative directions, their documented planning bearing little or no resemblance to the guidelines.

While keeping in mind frameworks, guidelines and initiatives, many schools attempt to focus and develop experiences which are meaningful, pupil-centred, pupil-initiated, creative, purposeful and enjoyable. You will be aware of the challenges these ideas present for organising and accounting for learning through long-term and medium-term planning approaches. Experienced teachers and schools are able to reflect on existing planning strategies and consider ways to maintain some flexibility and interest.

Planning in art and design

As intending teachers you will need to be familiar with approaches to, and processes of, planning. This section of the book presents an overview of the process, as schools work from initial ideas to more detailed plans. It is worth remembering that when visiting different schools, the planning for art and design may look different to that described here. However, the principles, once understood, can be used not only to make sense of existing planning but to produce independent plans.

Planning generally takes place through different stages, although the timescales of these planning stages vary depending on particular school 'planning review cycles'.

- *Long-term planning* applies to the whole school and covers all year groups, including the division of classes. Usually the art subject co-ordinator creates the long-term plan or it falls to the responsibility of a creative arts team. The plans tend to be reviewed every two–three years. This planning stage ensures coverage, progression and development.
- *Medium-term planning* occurs at a year group or class level. Medium-term plans are either completed by the art and design subject co-ordinator, the creative arts team, or written by the classroom teacher, or year teams in consultation with the art and design subject co-ordinator. The plans normally address projects or themes and extend over a half term or whole term period. The medium-term plan extends the coverage and progression suggested in the long-term plan to include more detail of art and design experiences, processes and materials involved. The detail will extend in some medium-term plans to an indication of the teaching programme, resources, assessment opportunities and health and safety issues. Good practice proposes these plans as working documents, annotated with reflective and evaluative notes.
- *Short-term planning* applies to individual classes. It usually covers a lesson per week and is generally reviewed weekly, directly following taught sessions. Short-term plans are written by class teachers and reflect the medium-term plans. They build on this material by advancing more specific learning intentions and objectives. Importantly they include a detailed teaching programme to support a series of progressive and developmental activities.

Long-term planning in art and design

Although the vast majority of schools have some form of long-term planning for art and design, the level of detail included and the way it is presented will vary. This presents your first challenge as you consider an overview of the planning approach. This section will illustrate the process of moving from initial themes to completed plans. The process takes into account the requirements of:

- school ethos;
- National Curriculum;
- coverage;
- progression;
- continuity;
- development;
- interest;
- resources.

A long-term overview should:

- reflect a year plan for all year groups in art and design with a progression of experience, processes and materials, with broad and balanced opportunities to access learning in the subject;
- be available to assist the development of medium-term planning;
- be consistent with the whole-school development plan, linked to the school annual curriculum plan and be agreed by all staff;
- present the provision for art and design per year for each year group or mixed-age class and where it occurs on the annual timetable;
- reflect the requirements for art and design for the appropriate key stage according to national frameworks and guidelines.

Organising a long-term plan

Schools work from their whole-school curriculum plans to develop 'themes' or topics. These tend to be shaped by other subject areas but can also be specific to art and design, for example, exploring a visual element or the work of an artist, craftsperson or designer.

The themes tend to be broadly grouped as:

- ourselves;
- our experiences;
- stories;
- natural forms;
- made objects;
- the local environment.

Themes are then extended and may include:

- myself;
- myself and others;
- light and shadow;
- local and distant environments;

- artists;
- near and distant cultures;
- history projects;
- Tudors;
- Greeks;
- Egyptians;
- Victorians;
- water;
- movement and the figure;
- visual elements;
- colour;
- line;
- pattern;
- shape;
- texture;
- form and space;
- machines;
- food;
- growth;
- space;
- celebrations and festivals.

REFLECTIVE TASK

Refer to a long-term plan obtained from a school. Many schools make these available on their websites. Identify the thematic approach taken, match themes to the broad themes identified above. Consider where these themes will make cross-curricular links.

Themes are then spread across the terms and may appear as in Figure 7.1, in what can be considered as an *initial long-term overview*.

Autumn 1 themes	R	1	2	3	4	5	6
	Mirror, mirror	Around the world	Texture	Town and country	Treasure Island	Victorians	Structures
Autumn 2 themes	Jack Frost	Starry, starry night	Machines	Mr Seahorse	Shape and pattern	The Greek Pottery Shop	Save the planet
Spring 1 themes	Robots	We are all going to the zoo tomorrow	All things bright and beautiful	Movement (art and D&T)	Let's animate	Fauvism	Midsummer Night's Dream
Spring 2 themes	Going to work	My school	A very long time ago	Colour	Sandwiches (art and D&T)	Paul Klee	
Summer 1 themes	Old MacDonald had a farm	The garden centre	The elements	Egyptians	Tudors	Water	Time
Summer 2 themes	Seaside	Crazy bug ball	Holidays	My pet shop	Out on the ocean	Landscapes	Journeys

Figure 7.1 Initial long-term overview at Somerville Primary School

From this position schools will create a more *developed* long-term overview by considering progression and coverage of experiences, processes and materials, visual elements, artists and pupil interest. Figure 7.2 represents a *developed* long-term overview.

CASE STUDY 7.1
Somerville Primary School

Somerville Primary School is situated in a small town.

The school has decided to use a thematic approach to their planning. Some of the themes are inspired by cross-curricular subjects, whereas other themes are based around art and design experiences and processes.

The planning is organised initially by the art and design subject co-ordinator, at the long-term planning stage. Suggestions for experiences and activities are provided for the medium-term plans, but all staff members prepare detailed medium-term planning in year teams, adapting ideas to meet the needs of their class. This approach maintains coverage and progression, broad and balanced experiences in two and three dimensions, whilst encouraging some flexibility and creativity.

This planning adopts the following characteristics.

- It enables a form of drawing and painting to be included in every project. This promotes drawing and painting as fundamental areas of experience to art and design learning.
- Experiences and processes include what are described as a major and minor focus.
- Something 2D is offered at least once a half term: collage, print or textiles.
- Something 3D is offered at least once a term: construction, modelling.
- Learning occurs individually, as small-group work or through whole-class collaboration.

REFLECTIVE TASK

You may come across a situation in school where there is no *developed long-term overview*. You may just be given a theme, similar to those described in Figure 7.2. You will see below how these themes are developed by schools following a procedure that establishes which experiences and processes are to be emphasised.

When preparing a *developed long-term overview*, teachers develop initial themes by considering:

- the aims and purposes of art and design, described by the EYFS profile, and the National Curriculum Key Stages 1 and 2;
- the school's policy for art and design and the subject's contribution to the whole primary curriculum;
- progression in the main art and design experiences across the school (these are: drawing, painting, collage, printmaking, textiles and sculpture, and lens-based media and ICT);
- major and minor focus areas, identifying key experiences and processes;
- coverage of visual elements: colour, line, pattern, shape, space, texture, form;
- how content may best be sequenced;
- the practicalities of organising the teaching of art and design, for example, which activities require more sustained time, what resources are available, how much budget is offered;

	R	1	2	3	4	5	6
Autumn 1 themes	Mirror, mirror	Around the world	Texture	Town and Country	Treasure Island	Victorians	Structures
Core experiences	Drawing m Painting	Drawing Painting	Drawing Painting **M**	Drawing **M** Painting	Drawing Painting **m**	Drawing Painting	Drawing **m** Painting
M= Major focus **m = minor focus**	Sculpture **M** (clay/salt dough)	Printing (found objects/rubbing) **M** Sculpture (clay/model magic) **m**	Printing (press) **m**	Printing (plasticene/card) **m** Sculpture (clay)	Printing (card) Textiles (flour resist/embellishment) **M**	Printing (press) **m** Textiles (stitching) **M**	Sculpture **M** (sticks/wire/tissue)
Artists	*van Eyck*	*Architects*	*Jasper Johns*	*Christo*	*Paul Cézanne*	*John Everett Millais*	*Barbara Hepworth*
Autumn 2 themes	Jack Frost	Starry, starry night	Machines	Mr Seahorse	Shape and pattern	The Greek Pottery Shop	Save the planet
Core experiences	Drawing Painting	Drawing Painting	Drawing Painting	Drawing Painting	Drawing Painting	Drawing Painting	Drawing Painting **m**
M= Major focus **m = minor focus**	Printing **M** Sculpture (pipe cleaners and foils) **m**	Printing (block/card) **m** Sculpture (card, foil and tissue) **M**	Textiles (weaving) **M** Sculpture (Clay) **m**	Collage **m** Sculpture (card papier-mâché) **M**	Collage **M** Sculpture (Clay) **m**	Printing (string) **m** Sculpture (clay) **M**	Collage/print **M**
Artists	*Photographs/ story books*	*van Gogh*	*Paolozzi*	*Eric Carle*	*Robert Delaunay/ Indian textiles*	*British Museum website*	*Photography museum*
Spring 1 themes	Robots	We are all going to the zoo tomorrow	All things bright and beautiful	Movement (art and D&T)	Let's animate	Fauvism	Midsummer Night's Dream
Core experiences	Drawing **m** Painting	Drawing Painting	Drawing Painting **M**	Drawing Painting **m**	Drawing Painting	Drawing Painting **M**	Drawing Painting **M**
M= Major focus **m = minor focus**	Printing sculpture (junk) **M**	Collage (furs) **m** Printing (hands) Textiles (sewing) **M** Sculpture (malleable)	Collage Textiles (dyes) **m**	Sculpture **M** (card figure on DT vehicle)	Sculpture (malleable) **m** ICT **M**	ICT **m**	Sculpture (clay) **m** ICT
Artists	*Story books*	*Franz Marc*	*Joan Miró*	*Roman patterns*	*Artworks/Nick Park*	*Matisse/Derain/ Vlaminck*	*Book illustrations*

	R	1	2	3	4	5	6
Spring 2 themes	Going to work	My school	A very long time ago	Colour	Sandwiches (art and D&T)	Paul Klee	Midsummer Night's Dream
Core experiences	Drawing Painting	Drawing Painting	Drawing Painting	Drawing Painting m	Drawing Painting m	**Drawing** Painting m	Drawing Painting M
M= Major focus **m = minor focus**	Collage Textiles (weaving) m Printing (fingers) M	Printing (rubbing) m Sculpture (pipe cleaner and wool) M	Sculpture (paper and paste) M	Textiles (Dyes and stitches) M	ICT M	Sculpture (mobiles-laminate) M	Sculpture (clay) m ICT
Artists	*Pablo Picasso*	*Georgia O'Keeffe*	*Art gallery sites*	*Kandinsky*			*Book illustrations*
Summer 1 themes	Old MacDonald had a farm	The garden centre	The elements	Egyptians	Tudors	Water	Time
Core experiences	Drawing Painting	Drawing Painting m	Drawing Painting m	Drawing Painting	Drawing Painting	Drawing Painting m	Drawing Painting
M= Major focus **m = minor focus**	Collage/card M Printing (mask) Sculpture (clay/plastic modelling) m	Collage M Textiles (weaving) m	Printing (press print) M	Printing (press) M Sculpture (recycling-bottles) m	Textiles (stitching) M Sculpture (malleable/jewellery) m	Textiles (dyes and stitches) M	Textiles/resist m Sculpture (mod roc) M
Artists			*Jane Ray: Illustrator*		*National Gallery visit*	*Hokusai*	
Summer 2 themes	Seaside	Crazy bug ball	Holidays	My pet shop	Out on the ocean	Landscapes	Journeys
Core experiences	Drawing Painting m	Drawing m Painting	Drawing Painting	Drawing Painting	Drawing Painting	Drawing Painting M	Drawing Painting M
M= Major focus **m = minor focus**	Collage, Sculpture (papier-mâché) M	Sculpture (junk) M	Textiles (weaving) M Printing (bubble) m	Collage Sculpture (card) M	Collage m Sculpture (mobiles/papers/laminates) M	Textiles (cut and stitch) m	Collage ICT m
Artists		*Picture books*			*Raoul Dufy*	*David Hockney*	*Kurt Schwitters*

Figure 7.2 A developed long-term plan overview at Somerville Primary School

- the balance between 2D and 3D work;
- opportunities for visits to museums, galleries and other sites;
- links with other curriculum areas;
- assessment opportunities.

As you look through this list compare Figure 7.1 with Figure 7.2. This will help maintain your understanding of how schools and teachers work from initial ideas and plans, to more developed and detailed plans. This awareness will help you when you are next in a school, to understand existing planning, and to develop plans which are presented to you as only initial themes or topics.

Medium-term planning

With long-term overviews completed, a school is in a position to translate this material in preparation for half term or full term projects or schemes of work. Some consideration will be given at this to point to making clearer links, where appropriate, to other subject areas, including timetabling and resource arrangements. These may include: considering schedules for room availability, coinciding taught material with material being taught in other subject areas, anticipating dates for excursions, or blocking time for a visiting artist.

As an intending teacher you will be required to prepare medium-term plans to extend over a number of weeks. It is normal for schools to follow the pattern of terms or half terms to determine the length of periods of study. We can anticipate these as being approximately seven weeks. Your school-based experiences may demand a period less than this. However, medium-term plans should ensure progression and development across a number, or sequence, of lessons. A sequence of three or four lessons would be determined as relatively short.

Formats for medium-term planning vary between schools and training institutions, each having their own expectations and requirements. However, in most cases medium-term plans include the following areas, to organise and structure progressive and developmental learning experiences:

- overall theme;
- broad objectives;
- National Curriculum references;
- key art and design experiences and processes;
- key visual elements;
- suggested artists, craftspeople or designers;
- sequenced suggested activities;
- assessment opportunities;
- vocabulary;
- resources;
- health and safety.

From an initial theme to a medium-term plan: example from Somerville Primary School

Somerville Primary School's Year 2 project on machines (Figure 7.3) is linked to a planned history project in the same term, exploring transport. The developed long-term overview

(Figure 7.2) identifies a number of key experiences in art and design: drawing, painting, textiles and sculpture for the machines project. Elsewhere we have heard that Somerville supports most projects with core experiences of drawing and painting. In addition they balance opportunities between major and minor experiences, two-dimensional and three-dimensional work. In this example textile work is described as a major focus and sculpture as minor (see Figure 7.2).

Understanding this level of provision from planning documentation is not always clear. Discussion and conversation with staff members will reveal sometimes hidden explanations. Schools do not hide information intentionally, but documentation procedures occasionally make assumptions which newcomers to that documentation find difficult to assimilate.

The machines topic builds on previous experiences and supports future learning in art and design. In this way it fits into a developed long-term plan, supporting coverage of appropriate experiences, processes, materials and skills. This not only serves to address a range of learning needs and children's strengths, but also provides an opportunity to try out a range of processes and experiences throughout the Early Years Foundation Stage and Key Stages 1 and 2.

Following discussion between teachers and the art and design subject co-ordinator, the machines topic is then presented as a scheme of work for the term, in the form of a medium-term plan. In this example Somerville Primary School has prepared work for a six-week period.

Short-term planning: developing lesson plans

Detailed and considered lesson plans support considered teaching and learning experiences. Although good planning does not guarantee good teaching it does provide an opportunity to think through the procedure, content and structure of a lesson. This helps teachers anticipate and make appropriate decisions, which in turn support learning. The decision making involves matching activities to learning objectives, inventing ways of starting lessons, matching resources to needs, offering support and challenge, and establishing boundaries and expectations (Eisner, 2002, see *Chapter 6: Considering teachers and teaching: practice*).

The distinguishing feature of a lesson plan is the detail evident in the teaching and learning programme, where many of these decisions are considered and described in the structure and content of the lesson. The plan will include carefully thought-through elements:

- title;
- aims;
- objectives;
- National Curriculum references;
- prior learning or experience;
- teaching and learning: structure and content; teaching approaches, differentiation;
- resources;
- assessment opportunities;
- vocabulary;
- health and safety;
- artists, craftspeople and designers;
- cross-curricular links.

Broad objectives	Suggested learning activities	Resources for support and extension	Vocabulary
1.Develop drawing skills using a variety of media.	• Use pencil to create a tonal range (2B/3B). • Make drawings of machines (made forms) that show detail and reflect qualities and visual elements (line/ tone/shade/pattern).	A range of pencils and sharpener. Range of machine/tool pieces. Magnifying glasses. Cartridge paper.	line tone shade pattern pencil machine scale large small
2. Mix and match colours, explore tint and shade. Know the names of primary, secondary and tertiary colours.	• Produce colour wheels and explore colour mixing using powder paints. (Collaborative large sections of a circle.) • Mix colours individually and record a palette in books. • Explore colour theory – use primary and secondary colours and talk about tertiary. • Explore tint (adding white) and shade (adding black). • Assemble collaborative large colour wheels. • Look at artists' work incorporating machines and colour, and talk about use of colour and shape (Robert Delaunay).	Powder paints (cyan, lemon and cerise). Poster paint (black and white). Range of brushes, water pots, water, palettes, paper towels, large cartridge paper, string (to draw a large circle). Delaunay images.	cyan lemon cerise colour wheel primary colour secondary colour tint tone Robert Delaunay orphism cubism
3/4. Explore and produce collaborative weaving.	• Produce collaborative weaving in groups on a bicycle wheel, or alternative, using a range of textures and materials (some provided by the children). • Explore and discuss weaving and materials made by machines. • Weave to create textures and patterns, add beads with threads. • Consider and apply knowledge of artists' use of colour.	Bicycle wheel, wools, fabrics, threads, beads, images of fabrics under a microscope, examples of weaving.	warp weft vocabulary of textures of materials (woolly, shiny, silky etc.) warm colours cool colours complementary colours.
5/6. Exploring three dimensions and mark-making in clay.	• Look at images of Eduardo Paolozzi's machine-like sculptures, discuss what they are made of and introduce the idea of 'imaginative machines'. • Using black and white pastels and sugar paper draw individual machines. • Select a section of their machines to make a piece of small group machines in clay. • Use a range of tools and forms to cut, shape and impress patterns and textures into clay. • Arrange and photograph. • Talk about their sculptures and relate them to those of the artists studied.	Eduardo Paolozzi images. Black and white pastels, sugar paper, clay, tools, clay boards, cameras.	Eduardo Paolozzi machines surface form shape impress texture emboss
6/7. Evaluation and presentation.	• Discuss the work produced while considering slide show of images, including children's comments. • Evaluate and record comments in sketchbook.	Sketchbook. Glue. Slide show images.	presentation

Figure 7.3. Somerville Primary School medium-term plan for machines, Year 2, Autumn 2

REFLECTIVE TASK
REFLECTIVE TASK

Preparing a lesson plan is not always straightforward. In situations where you are working from detailed medium-term plans, some material can be transferred relatively easily. In other situations, to develop an approach to lesson planning you will need to draw on your own experiences, work from books, talk to your peers and colleagues, and work alongside tutors. Working within a suitably flexible framework will support the planning process. Look at the example in Figure 7.4. Compare this with your own experiences of planning and consider carefully your confidence in completing each area. Are you comfortable with what to include in each section?

Date	Year group	Title of project	National Curriculum references
Aims of the project	Overall summary of project.		
Learning objectives	Intended learning for children: processes, knowledge, skills or values.		
Prior learning and experience	Prior experiences and learning from unit of work or previous year group experiences.		

Teaching and learning: structure and content	Teaching approaches	Differentiation
Structured experiences and activities identified for children. Supporting and challenging interventions from teachers: • Starting ideas. • Helping children explore and develop ideas. • Supporting ideas. • Helping children investigate and make. • Developing ideas. • Helping children review and develop ideas. • Reviewing and presenting ideas. • Helping children understand the visual, tactile and spatial qualities of art and design. • Helping children understand the work of others. Ways of organising classroom and learning opportunities: individual, paired or group work, large and small scale.	Opening strategies Organisational strategies Instructional strategies Motivational strategies Questioning strategies Closing strategies (Burton, 2001)	Different and varied resources and interventions to support and challenge pupils' learning.

Resources Materials and resources for teaching and learning, including ICT.
Assessment opportunities Opportunities to identify learning, during the process of, and following, experiences and activities: through conversations, in sketchbooks, in finished work, between children and adults, between children and children, as individuals.
Health and safety: Risk assessment.

Artists, craftspeople, designers to be used	Cross-curricular links

Figure 7.4 Example lesson plan format

Developing the contents of a lesson plan

Most approaches to short-term lesson planning include areas as identified above, although you will find some variations around these themes.

Title

This will include:

- class and year group, date of lesson;
- links to National Curriculum for art and design or EYFS profile.

Aims

This statement links the lesson to the documented long-term and medium-term plans, indicating a broad area of study and appropriate experiences and processes. The aims tend to cover several lessons, and possibly the whole project; as such, particular lessons support the broader aims, usually expressed through objectives.

National Curriculum references

Reflecting National Curriculum references identified in the medium-term plan.

Prior learning or experience

This places the lesson with previous learning, in the context of the medium-term plan.

Learning objectives

Objectives are statements used to describe learning, which the lesson hopes to support and develop. Objectives usually refer to learning in terms of processes, knowledge, skills or values.

PRACTICAL TASK PRACTICAL TASK **PRACTICAL TASK** PRACTICAL TASK **PRACTICAL TASK**

Developing and recording objectives

Developing and recording objectives can be a challenging and time-consuming procedure. It involves a process of considering how an activity supports a particular aspect of learning: possibly skill development, knowledge about a material or a process, knowledge of the work of an artist, or the promotion of particular values.

However, when developing and recording objectives for planning purposes, there is no *magic pot* of objectives to turn to. It is useful to think initially in terms of positive verbs or 'stem verbs'. These provide the 'root' of the objective statement. For example the following verbs would prove useful 'stem verbs' for art and design:

- analyse
- combine
- communicate
- compare
- create
- decorate

- express
- identify
- invent
- know
- make
- observe

- demonstrate
- discover
- embellish
- evaluate
- examine
- explore

- record
- research
- review
- select
- sustain
- understand

As an example, a lesson aimed at developing children's abilities to record from first-hand observation qualities of surface and texture, stem verbs would form the root of the following objectives.

Children will be able to:

- *identify*, *select* and *compare* areas of texture in natural objects;
- *make* observational drawings from close up;
- *combine* two *materials* to show different textures;
- *examine* and *compare* artists' use of materials to show texture;
- *demonstrate* understanding with increased vocabulary.

Refer to the list of verbs, add some of your own and record the 'root' phrases of objectives.

Refer to *Chapter 5: Considering teachers and teaching: principles* and read the description of the lesson taught by Ms Evans. Develop and record four objectives for this lesson, using stem verbs as the root phrases and keeping in mind learning areas of skill development, knowledge, processes and values.

In some cases you may find criticism levelled at objectives suggesting they describe activities rather than learning, for example *make observational drawings from close up*, could be considered an activity. In many ways it is, but as learning in art and design is *active* it is almost unavoidable. The objective can be developed further by adding *combine two materials to show different textures*, which adds detail to the learning and offers a level of requirement and expectation in terms of the *close-up drawings*.

Teaching and learning: structure and content

There is no official way of organising teaching and learning in art and design. However, as you build towards a more experienced position, it remains useful to consider phases of lessons. The phases of a lesson can be indicated by describing them as an *introduction*, a period of *development* and a *conclusion*. Not all lessons follow such rigid sequential development, but they are good starting points for organising thoughts about teaching, as you consider phases through which you can support children.

Introduction
- Starting ideas.
- Helping children explore and develop ideas.
- Supporting ideas.

Development
- Developing ideas.
- Helping children investigate and make.

Conclusions
- Reviewing and presenting ideas.
- Helping children reflect on and develop ideas.

Spread across the phases will be periods of time where you introduce, explain, demonstrate, show examples, listen to poems, ask for suggestions, prompt investigation, challenge, invite, review, suggest alternatives, highlight potential of materials.

It is useful to ask yourself, 'How am I helping children towards the learning described in the objectives?'

How am I...
- helping children understand art and design experiences, processes and materials?
- helping children understand the visual, tactile and spatial qualities of art and design?
- helping children understand the work of others?

Introduction
The introductory part of a lesson may involve discussion; it may introduce something completely new or build on a previous experience; it may start with an activity; it may involve listening to a poem or watching a dance; it may involve sharing the intentions of the lesson or recording objectives on a board. When preparing the lesson plan you will be able to make good use of the 'stem verbs' described above. These can be used to highlight your teaching role, for example, to start a lesson you could:

- *read* a story;
- *show* a range of postcards;
- *ask* children to identify similarities and differences;
- *take* children on a walk;
- *ask* children to notice all things that are green;
- *challenge* children to explore materials for three minutes;
- *provide* a range of textures and surfaces in a 'feely bag'.

REFLECTIVE TASK

Read the following and consider how the teacher makes a purposeful start to a lesson by building on previous experience, and engaging the children in an interesting *introduction* activity.

Zoe's Year 5 class had been on a visit to a sculpture park for an afternoon last week. She wanted to see what had stayed in their minds the next art and design lesson. Zoe prepared a montage of photographs of the sculptures they had seen and experienced. She divided the class into groups of three children. She asked the children to discuss the sculptures in their groups, using words to describe the sculpture's appearance, construction or what the sculpture reminded them of when they were in the sculpture park. These ideas were quickly recorded in note form, and then reported to the class. This prompted a class discussion and enabled Zoe to speculate about individual engagement. This introduction supported the initial learning objectives for the lesson, which were:

- to discuss ideas about sculptures that were in the park;
- to design two ideas for their own sculpture.

Development
The development of a lesson will involve you and the children in the core activities of art and design:

- investigating materials;
- experimenting with tools and processes;
- developing and applying skills;
- exploring and researching artists;
- developing awareness of visual elements;
- planning and designing with materials and ideas.

As lessons progress, an appropriate amount of time should be given over to children developing knowledge, skills and understanding. Plans should provide opportunities for children to engage in interesting activities which are hands-on and where children are encouraged to 'have a go'. For example children may be encouraged to explore paint, getting used to its properties, or exploring and blending oil pastels. Increased experiences and opportunities help children to familiarise and adapt to an experience, process, or material. From this point children are in a better position to understand and work with materials, tools and processes in their own creative and inventive ways.

Lesson plans support development by identifying roles for teachers and children where teachers:

- demonstrate techniques;
- encourage children to use sketchbooks to try things out;
- show examples of artists' sketchbooks;
- explore material properties with children;
- challenge children to select and combine materials;
- guide children towards selecting or combining materials;
- suggest alternatives;
- question children about their choices;
- value children's responses;
- provide examples of material use or techniques by other artists, craftspeople or designers;
- discuss the range of responses in the class;
- organise materials for accessibility.

Conclusion

Not all lessons in art and design will see the completion of practical work. However, a concluding period provides time for children to reflect on their learning and progress during the lesson. It might be that the teacher asks children to set themselves targets at the beginning of a lesson, or that objectives are used to focus concluding reviews. The format for conclusions can involve whole-class activity, or small groups sharing their work around a table, reflecting on achievements and identifying future developmental targets. Teachers may seek to find evidence of children demonstrating understanding of key lesson themes through the appropriate use of vocabulary.

Lesson plans support concluding periods of review and evaluation by identifying where teachers:

- listen carefully to responses;
- provide vocabulary charts to support responses;
- share ideas with others;
- suggest criteria for evaluating work;
- record observations of artists' work;

- suggest a change in scale;
- scan work and project it via the data projector;
- make notes alongside the projected image;
- record and document processes of working with photographs and words;
- encourage children to document and review their own process of working with words and photographs.

Within the structure and content of the teaching and learning part of a lesson plan you will also have an opportunity to indicate how you will organise children and activities: individual, paired or group work, on a large or small scale.

PRACTICAL TASK PRACTICAL TASK **PRACTICAL TASK** PRACTICAL TASK **PRACTICAL TASK**

Selecting appropriate learning experiences and activities

The activities and experiences which make up the active and experiential part of an art and design lesson, the essence of art and design, are not always easily envisaged. You may find yourself in a position working alongside an experienced teacher, who shares many activities with you. In other situations the medium-term plan will indicate what activities to plan for and resource. To support and develop existing ideas, or think of new ones, you will need to be receptive to possibilities. Refer to the themes presented in Figure 7.2 and think about activities to support learning. To stimulate and develop a range of ideas: visit galleries for inspiration; talk to teachers; look at the work of children in schools; make use of published 'ideas' books; visit the NSEAD website; or look through *Start* (NSEAD), the primary art and design magazine; look in children's picture books; browse the internet; or visit a museum.

Differentiation

As you work through the detail of the structure and content of the lesson plan in a considered way, you will be in a position to play close attention to differentiated needs. For some children this may mean supporting with alternative resources and materials, providing an activity in three dimensions rather than two, providing exemplar material, or modifying a challenge. It may be useful to sit with a group, offering further explanations or more direct intervention, helping children to see and realise visual qualities with 'directed looking'. 'Have you noticed that shape, what does it remind you of? How would you describe those lines? Can you select a material to match this surface texture?'

Resources

Thinking ahead about activities will inevitably lead you to thinking about resources to stimulate and support learning. During the planning process you are advised to list these in a detailed way, anticipating your needs very carefully. It will also be useful to record in the plan any relevant detail concerning the distribution of resources, as a classroom management consideration.

REFLECTIVE TASK

Think about the resources needed to support art and design lessons, lessons you have observed or those described in this book. Where would you obtain resources from, beyond those available in schools? Resources can be bought from specialist companies or found more cheaply by taking advantage of recycling opportunities. Libraries, galleries and museums also offer resources to support learning. Think about other adults supporting learning, and investigate local networks for possible artists, designers and craftspeople willing to share expertise and knowledge alongside children. Consider local galleries and museums, and identify education officers and their education programmes.

Assessment opportunities

As an integral part of teaching and learning, assessment opportunities form an important part of lesson plans. As suggested in *Chapter 8: Assessment, monitoring and feedback*, opportunities for assessment should be focused:

- during activities;
- following short periods of activity;
- following longer periods of activity.

Lesson plans will enable a more targeted approach to assessment. This detail at the planning stage will encourage you to:

- *identify* focus groups of children;
- *consider* appropriate recording procedures;
- *target* questions to support assessment;
- *consider* and *share* criteria for success, built from objectives;
- *identify* opportunities to talk to children;
- *identify* opportunities for children to explore ideas in sketchbooks.

Vocabulary

Elsewhere in this book (*Chapter 4: Knowledge and understanding: progression of experiences and processes*, *Chapter 5: Teachers and teaching: principles*) we have indicated that vocabulary supports and develops learning in art and design. Talking to children about their work, about visual, spatial and tactile qualities, about processes and materials, about the work of other artists, in a positive and purposeful way encourages a purposeful and positive approach to the subject. Helping children to articulate their work, using developed vocabulary, is not a substitute for developing their visual, spatial or tactile art and design vocabulary. The way people express their ideas graphically or through paint, or through modelling materials should not be substituted with words, but they can make an important contribution to the learning and teaching process.

During the planning process identify key language related to process and materials, and think imaginatively to describe the visual, spatial and tactile qualities of art and design.

Lesson plans can be used to:
- *identify* key vocabulary;
- *identify* imaginative vocabulary;
- *identify* opportunities to share vocabulary;
- *encourage* children to use and develop vocabulary;
- *consider* ways of recording and presenting vocabulary.

Health and safety

All classroom practices should follow good procedures in terms of health and safety. It is important that you consider the requirements of the school, local authority and national frameworks. As a student teacher going into schools on school experience it is vital to take advice from mentors, teachers, head teachers, and health and safety officers regarding activities and requirements for different art and design experiences. Always ask for, and follow, the risk assessment procedure in a school for any skill or activity which has potential risks.

The NSEAD has excellent guidance on their website: www.nsead.org/home/index.aspx

Although most materials and experiences adopted by primary schools use safe procedures and non-toxic materials, the lesson plan should indicate clearly that you have considered appropriately any health and safety issues.

Artists, craftspeople and designers

Considering appropriate artists, craftspeople and designers to support and develop experiences and processes is appropriate at the planning stage. This can be supported by referring to books, visiting galleries and museums, talking to colleagues or visiting online sources.

If you are intending to use an artist, craftsperson or designer's work as an integral part of a lesson you will need to plan carefully this opportunity.

Lesson plans support the considered use of artists, craftspeople and designers, offering opportunities for teachers and children to:

- *identify* appropriate and varied artists, craftspeople and designers;
- *identify* and *explore* similarities and differences in artists' work;
- *extend* the range of artists, craftspeople and designers;
- *use* themes to connect artists, craftspeople and designers;
- *identify* strategies to *engage* children with images and artefacts.

Cross-curricular links

Clear links may be made to other subject areas within the national frameworks and curriculum guidelines. This may extend to broader areas of learning including key skills, thinking skills or personal, spiritual, moral, social and cultural development, suggested in the National Curriculum (DfEE, 1999). Making links to other subjects can be exciting, supporting and developing learning *in* or *through* art and design.

REFLECTIVE TASK

Consider the case study below, Magic carpets, describing a planning process which engages the ideas of children. Increasingly this approach is found in early years settings, and some Key Stage 1 environments, where children track and follow their own learning journeys.

CASE STUDY 7.2

Magic carpets

Mrs Barker involved her Year 1 class in the planning for a 'magic carpet' project. Working alongside each other, listening and sharing their ideas, the children make many suggestions. Mrs Barker stimulates some of the discussion by sharing objects, showing pictures, telling stories and asking open questions. She reads a magic carpet poem, with rhyming couplets, which the class soon begin to join in with.

The class also agree on some questions to find out more about magic carpets:

1. Do any other stories and poems feature magic carpets?
2. What artists have used magic carpets in their compositions?
3. Where do the patterns for carpets come from?
4. Who makes a carpet or rug, and how are they made?

The class also plan how they will find out about magic carpets, and they suggest that they could:

● use the internet at home and school;
● look in the school and town libraries for books;
● look for films at home;
● visit a rug shop;
● look at patterns on carpets and rugs at home.

Mrs Barker turns the class's attention to some images of decorative patterns used in rug and carpet making. She prompts the children to think about art and design activities which could explore the patterns further or the qualities of rugs. The children suggest they could:

1. make their own rug;
2. make up their own rug or carpet pattern or design;
3. go for an adventure on an imaginary magic carpet.

Mrs Barker takes the suggestions away. She meets the other Year 1 class teacher and they pool together their ideas. They then consider activities and materials to support the children's ideas. These are established alongside the National Curriculum and reflect previous art and design learning experiences.

PRACTICAL TASK PRACTICAL TASK **PRACTICAL TASK** PRACTICAL TASK **PRACTICAL TASK**

Self-evaluation

Look at and consider Figure 7.5 on page 126.

Consider your development needs in terms of planning for art and design in primary schools, with reference to the *continuum of experience, needs, confidence and support* detailed in the *Introduction* and developed in *Chapter 5: Considering teachers and teaching: principles.*

	Introductory	Threshold	Post-threshold
Long-term planning	Work alongside teachers to understand existing planning. Identify the range of experiences, processes and activities on the plans. Consider ideas suitable to age group.	Work alongside class teachers to understand existing planning. Offer some ideas about the planning that exists and suggest how these could be developed into short projects.	Work alongside class teachers to understand existing planning. Offer some ideas about the planning that exists and suggest how these could be developed into short projects.
Medium-term planning	Plan a project working closely with the class teacher. Organise clear objectives and aims. Plan a range of experiences and processes with guidance from the class teacher. Check resources are available.	Create planning independently but with some discussion with the class teacher. Demonstrate an understanding of planning a sequence of lessons that ensures coverage and progression. Organise resources and plan management for the lessons.	Organise a sequence of lessons after clarification of the school's art and design long-term plan. Plan activities that ensure coverage of experiences and processes, together with progression and creativity. Plan resources, select a variety of materials and stimuli and organise for effective classroom management.
Short-term planning	Plan a lesson with close guidance from the class teacher. Present clear aims and objectives. Plan in a structured way to include introduction, development and conclusion. Plan for evaluation and reflection.	Prepare short-term planning to fit into the sequence of previous and future lessons with the support of the class teacher. Present clear aims and objectives incorporating high expectations and challenges. Plan for assessment opportunities during and following activities.	Prepare lesson plans independently, with imaginative activities, linked to previous and future lessons. Plan teaching interventions that anticipate differentiated needs.

Figure 7.5 Planning for art and design: self evaluation

A SUMMARY OF **KEY POINTS**

In this chapter we have explored:

> **the planning process in art and design;**

> **developmental approaches to planning;**

> **the links between different planning phases;**

> **detail of content to be included in planning phases;**

> **lesson plans as a source of considered decision making.**

MOVING *ON* > > > > > > MOVING *ON* > > > > > > MOVING *ON*

Planning involves a range of phases, and is dependent in many ways on experience and expertise. Identify areas within planning arrangements where you need to prioritise your own professional development. Collect and refer to planning documentation to support these needs. Do so in a structured way which helps you identify the formation of a plan, and as such, understand it better.

REFERENCES REFERENCES **REFERENCES** REFERENCES **REFERENCES** REFERENCES

Burton, D (2001) How do we teach? Results of a National Survey of Instruction in Secondary Art Education. *Studies in Art Education: A journal of issues and research*, 42 (2): 131–45.

DCSF (2008) *Early Years Foundation Stage Statutory Framework*. Nottingham: DCSF Publications.

DfEE (1999) *The National Curriculum*. London: HMSO.

QCA (2000) *Art and design: Scheme of work for Key Stages 1 and 2*. Sudbury: QCA.

QCA (2008) E*arly Years Foundation Stage Profile Handbook*. London: HMSO.

FURTHER READING FURTHER READING **FURTHER READING** FURTHER READING

Barnes, R (2006) *Teaching art to young children 4–9*, 2nd edn. Abingdon: RoutledgeFalmer.

www.nsead.org.uk

The website for the National Society for Education in Art and Design. Representing art education, this is an excellent site for all manner of enquiries, from buying books to courses for teachers, including *Start*, the primary art and design magazine.

8
Assessment, monitoring and feedback

Chapter objectives

By the end of this chapter you will have:

- **broadened your awareness and understanding of assessment in art and design;**
- **developed your understanding of assessment strategies in art and design;**
- **developed your awareness of the value and use of evaluation and feedback;**
- **developed your awareness of progression and expectations in art and design.**

This chapter addresses the following Standards for QTS: **Q4, Q11, Q12, Q27, Q28.**

Key themes: assessment; evaluation; monitoring; reporting; feedback; development; documentation; progression.

Introduction

Seen positively, assessment in art and design can make a valuable contribution to children's creative and artistic development. Although this process is not always straightforward, offering direction and support to children during and after their learning is an integral and important part of any curriculum design and teaching approach. Assessment can become a less positive experience or exceed its usefulness when it:

- dominates creative thinking about teaching;
- dictates the outcomes of art lessons, in that they must be 'measurable';
- talks about the creative and artistic process in only mechanical terms, overlooking the human endeavour of such activity;
- presents assessment statements as part of a deficit model, rather than supporting current achievements.

This chapter will help you approach assessment in art and design in ways which are supportive, positive, flexible, useful and worthwhile.

Overcoming concerns about assessment and the arts

Eisner (2002, p178) reminds us of the sometimes 'uneasy' relationship between arts education and assessment and evaluation (a distinction is made between assessment as a process of reviewing and appraising student work and evaluation as the appraisal of curriculum materials and teaching approaches). He suggests several reasons for this potentially uncomfortable relationship, which we outline below.

Judgements are seen to restrict creative potential

This is a very common argument, cited against the use of assessment strategies in art and design. It suggests that any intervention from another person will impede an individual's creative will, and in some way stifle expressive art work. Many art and design educators have adopted this approach to assessment, preferring to stand back and acknowledge the work of individuals as indicators of personal creative expression. However, you will also know that we have considered learning as a social activity based on the relationships with others and the environments in which learning can take place. Just as adult artists do, children can share ideas with others, draw on previous experiences and build on their evolving skill development, knowledge and understanding. The skilled teacher realises the context of the work being produced and offers constructive and sensitive feedback. This feedback supports motivation; it supports knowledge and skill development; it supports pupil self-evaluation skills and it can support the processes of learning as well as the outcomes.

Attempts to measure things are incompatible with the arts

Measuring and determining a level of performance against a set of indicative statements sounds almost antithetical to creative arts activity. It would be a poor educational experience which only set out to teach what could be measured in such crude or mechanical terms. Experiences of measuring in schools over the past 15 years or so have been governed by experiences of testing against national standards in standardised tests, in an attempt to level and report pupil attainment in a spread of National Curriculum subjects. However, teachers have also maintained assessment strategies which do better than measure against norms. They integrate assessment into the process of learning and teaching.

Assessment strategies in art and design can also do better than 'measure'; they can support learning by offering feedback, and accepting the responsibility of making judgements of value.

Assessment tends to focus on the product and overlook the process

The artistic process is often championed as being the crucial aspect of creative activity; you will hear artists from all sorts of backgrounds talking enthusiastically about the value of the process of working. This process involves exploring, inventing, trying things out, starting again, working things through, testing ideas, or experimenting with new combinations. Despite such value and importance, there has been a tendency to appraise the products of such activity out of context from this process and to see the products in isolation. As such, judgements are made against final criteria which overlook the fruitful and significant engagement with the learning process.

Assessment opportunities can be developed to support and appraise artistic and creative processes. Comments can be made about the level of motivation a pupil has had, their willingness to try new things, to take on board ideas, and to review their own work. Feedback can be focused on a pupil's flexibility and imagination in solving problems or imagining new ones, or on sustained concentration during the overcoming of technical difficulties. Eisner reminds us to keep in mind the products pupils produce as 'further markers along a journey' (Eisner, 2002, p181), in that objects and images, produced in art and design, are not necessarily end points, but extensions of the learning process: points of departure for new and interesting developments.

Assessment results in grading

There are some situations where offering a final statement about the quality of work may be appropriate and lead to some sort of grade. For example, schools which make use of the National Curriculum Attainment Targets and Level Descriptors (supported by the QCA) may find themselves working with a form of grading or levelling procedure. If a level is awarded for overall performance, for example a pupil may be described as achieving level 3 in their art and design work, this reports very little about the detail of their creative and artistic abilities. An overall level needs supporting with further description and detail, accounting for particular skill development, creative approaches to artistic processes of investigation and exploration, knowledge of materials and techniques and application of knowledge to particular problems and experiments. In other words, the breadth of the National Curriculum needs reporting in addition to a single grade or level.

Furthermore, the experience of working in art and design reminds us that things are made from parts, and that whole things may exceed or fall short of the sum of those parts. Teachers can comment on those parts, make judgements about them, support them with written and verbal feedback, encourage self-evaluation of the parts, but should not feel obliged to offer a grade or level description of each individual part, at each stage of artistic activity.

Establishing a positive and useful assessment experience

To support a positive and useful approach to assessment you should aim to establish an approach which encourages:

- creative thinking about teaching;
- flexible and varied processes and outcomes of art and design lessons;
- feedback about the creative and artistic process in terms which acknowledge the human endeavour of such activity;
- assessment statements which support current achievements, and indicate possible further developments.

REFLECTIVE TASK

Consider your own experiences of assessment, as a learner and as a teacher. Identify, where you can, assessment strategies which support your personal or academic or professional development. How was feedback given to you? Were you in a position to respond to feedback immediately or has your response been more measured, developing over a period of time? How have you responded to feedback which appears critical? Have you observed children responding positively to feedback? How have teachers supported children's development when answers or suggestions have been deemed wrong or misunderstood?

Assessment opportunities

Chapter 3: Considering learners and learning: principles and practice encouraged you to think about learning in art and design as an active and reflective process where ideas, impulses and feelings are transformed, connected and developed, through creative activity. It is important to remember that this process takes time. It benefits from space in which ideas grow and become increasingly sophisticated.

Assessment opportunities need to be mindful of this. Remember that:

1. judgement and feedback can be short and long term;
2. response to feedback may not always be immediate;
3. feedback can direct children to making long- and short-term connections.

Opportunities for assessment may be found during the process of working, at the end of a period of working, or following an extended period of working:

During the process of working: Ongoing assessment opportunities need to be managed in a reasonably systematic way, perhaps moving from table to table or group to group. This approach to *formative* assessment involves identifying areas of interest in work, examples of success or achievement, good examples of invention or creativity. The feedback can be directed to individuals and related to previous work or past experiences.

Following a period of working: The process of reviewing work is common to many curriculum areas; it asks adults and children to summarise progress and offer feedback on progress made. Statements to the whole class can be used to motivate further work, or more focused comments can target areas of development for individuals. It is unlikely that covering all children during this type of review will be possible, or indeed sensible. This is a good opportunity for children to engage in periods of self-evaluation and review, perhaps annotating copies of work in sketchbooks, with evaluative and reflective comments, supported by teacher examples, or through the use of 'word banks' to support a more developed vocabulary.

Following extended periods of work: There are opportunities for assessment following sustained periods of work, or at the end of a topic or series of themed lessons. It is more likely that this form of assessment will make *summative* statements about achievements and it may be that levelling indicators are used at this stage – although this information should be used with discretion in the support of further learning.

Assessment opportunities may take place with individuals, or groups, the whole class, or sometimes across year groups. They involve conversations, observations and discussions around work, the use of level descriptors, judgements and feedback. Feedback can be verbal or written, and conversations may take place between children and their peers, with 'partners' or groups, or with teachers and other adults.

Figure 8.1 Evidence of children learning in art and design can be found during the processes of making and in their final products – children will articulate understanding in their work, and through reflective evaluations

Assessment opportunities

Processes

Where do pupils:

- investigate new materials?
- combine materials in inventive and new ways?
- create unusual and imaginative responses?
- explore their ideas?
- challenge their own solutions?
- test out their understanding?
- investigate visual qualities?
- make connections?
- reflect on decisions?
- ask questions?

Use of materials

Where do pupils:

- select materials and tools?
- control materials and tools?
- manipulate materials and tools?
- combine materials and tools?
- organise materials and tools?

Evaluation and review

Where do pupils:

- identify visual, tactile and spatial qualities?
- refer to qualities with appropriate language?
- edit, adjust or adapt their work?
- adopt techniques of others?
- observe and notice differences or similarities?
- state preferences and dislikes?
- ask questions?

Whole class, groups, individuals

Mysterious shadows

There is a sense of excitement and intrigue as the children come back into the classroom following the lunchtime break. The room is dark and lit predominantly by candles and low-wattage spotlights. Everyday kitchen and household objects are suspended within the beams and flickering light, casting mysterious shadows across very large pieces of crisp white paper. The children are manoeuvred gently across the beams of light, their shadows cast against the walls. Unusually for an art lesson the teacher has asked the children to remain silent in this strangely-lit classroom atmosphere. The Year 4 children can barely contain themselves. 'You'll remember over the past few weeks we've been talking about light in science and religious studies, and learning about some of its properties.... Who can remember what we did in art last week?...which was connected to our theme of light?' Two or three hands go up 'Did we do some drawings with light bits and dark bits...with those messy chalk things?'

The lesson moves quickly to the shadows, and referring back to the previous sessions on light and tone the children are given a choice of charcoal or graphite pencils to produce their own 'shadow drawings'. The teacher demonstrates how to vary pressure and type of mark to control the quality and range of tone, recapping on skills from the previous week.

Working alongside a classroom assistant, two parent helpers, a student teacher and the teacher, the groups are organised at tables and make tentative beginnings on the large white sheets of paper to capture the qualities of the shadows. Approaches to the drawings are reserved and tentative. The teacher stops the class, gathers them together, and turns on the data projector. The intensity of its light is exaggerated in the darkened room. A collection of images is shown, some taken by the teacher of shadows around her home and shadows reflected light on walls, and images from the work of artists exploring light: van Gogh's *Potato Eaters*, and Cornellia Parker's *30 Pieces of Silver*. 'They look like silver wheels, silver coins...is that their shadow on the floor?...Look at that Miss, those shadows are massive.'

Just before the children return to their work, she highlights some features of the drawings so far, holding up examples of 'good use of tonal range...good use of marks to create tone...and a lovely sense of the mysterious shadows'.

Figure 8.2 Assessment opportunities in the session, 'mysterious shadows'

Indicators of success

Pupil level of engagement can be described as:

- willing;
- consistent;
- independent;
- enthusiastic;
- careful;
- imaginative;
- engaged for sustained periods;
- thoughtful;

- careful;
- consistent;
- independent;
- systematic;
- playful;
- inventive;
- deliberate;
- considered;
- knowledgeable;

- thoughtful;
- considerate;
- sensitive;
- aware;
- alert;
- able to make use of developed language
- knowledgeable.

During process
Following period of work
Following extended period of work

Focusing assessment

Directing assessment towards experiences is a useful approach, and one which attempts to take its lead from children, and their learning. In *Chapter 3: Considering learners and learning: principles and practice* learning was accounted for in a number of different ways, all of which provide focus for assessment activity, helping assessment remain an integral part of teaching.

You will be aware that learning can be organised in terms of processes, knowledge, skills and values. Opportunities exist to focus assessment support on the way children engage with artistic and creative processes, how they use knowledge and skills to engage with art experiences and materials, how they develop and use knowledge of artists to inform their own work and make judgements about the work of others.

Assessing processes

It is particularly important to seek out opportunities to comment on and support the learning process involved in art and design. During this process you will see children investigate, explore, try things out, test out ideas, create, invent, imagine, review and evaluate. You will be able to support this process by identifying when, and judging how well, pupils:

- investigate new materials;
- combine materials in inventive and new ways;
- create unusual and imaginative responses;
- explore their ideas;
- challenge their own solutions;
- test out their understanding;
- investigate visual qualities;
- make connections;
- reflect on decisions;
- ask questions.

You can add to your assessments that pupils do these things well when they are:

- willing;
- consistent;
- independent;
- enthusiastic;
- careful;
- imaginative;
- engaged for sustained periods;
- thoughtful.

Assessing the use of materials

Children learn to use materials to articulate ideas, impulses and feelings through their artistic images, objects, sounds and gestures. To develop these responses, and to develop their visual, tactile and spatial solutions, children need support from teachers. Feedback provides part of that support and helps children consider their application of skills and their under-standing of materials and techniques.

You will be able to support this aspect of art and design during and after activity by identifying when, and how well, pupils:

- select materials and tools;
- control materials and tools;
- manipulate materials and tools;
- combine materials and tools;
- organise materials and tools;
- transform materials and tools.

You can add to your assessments that pupils do these things well when they are:

- careful;
- consistent;
- independent;
- systematic;
- playful;
- inventive;
- deliberate;
- considered;
- knowledgeable.

Assessing evaluation and review of own and others' work

The National Curriculum encourages children to review and develop their own work, and to develop their awareness of the work of others. Supporting this sort of review and evaluation is a skilled activity, dependent on teacher interventions which integrate a variety of assessment approaches through prompts, questions and cues. During and after this process you will be able to identify when, and how well, pupils:

- identify visual, tactile and spatial qualities;
- refer to qualities with appropriate language;
- adapt techniques of others;
- edit, adjust or adapt their work;
- adopt techniques of others;
- observe and notice differences or similarities;
- state preferences and dislikes;
- adjust and modify preferences and dislikes;
- ask questions.

You can add to your assessments that pupils do these things well when they are:

- thoughtful;
- considerate;
- sensitive;
- aware;
- alert;
- able to make use of developed language;
- knowledgeable.

Providing feedback

The detail above provides a useful framework for providing feedback to pupils at different points during the development of work. For example you will be able to make comments about work which could be constructed along the following lines:

- You investigate visual qualities of line and tone with enthusiasm and imagination.
- You have combined materials in inventive ways, and considered your choice of materials carefully.
- You have thought about your own ideas independently, and made some imaginative adaptations.
- You have identified similarities in the work of different landscape artists in a knowledgeable way, making use of a developed vocabulary to describe their work.

This sort of feedback (DCSF, 2008) we could describe as being specific and positive. It identifies particular aspects of work and comments on them positively. In terms of providing feedback this is a very useful and targeted approach, which sits amongst other less focused forms of feedback. This variety can be described as:

Negative non-specific: negative comments which lack focus, and provide no opportunity for children to develop. *Avoid making statements like*:

- You have not worked well today and will need to try much harder next time.
- Your work is not of a quality we would expect in this class.

Negative specific: negative comments with some focus, but no supporting suggestions for development. *Avoid making statements like*:

- Your work lacks any real imagination.
- Your sense of texture is limited by your choice of materials.

Positive non-specific: positive comments which generally support a positive classroom atmosphere and encourage individual responses, but offer limited direct developmental support. *Make appropriate use of statements like*:

- Well done – you have all worked well today.
- A good art lesson – you have produced some interesting work.

Positive specific: positive and focused providing encouragement and direction for further development. *Make extensive use of statements like the following.*

- Your application of paint is controlled and shows good awareness of colour mixing. Consider using thinner layers of translucent paint to add depth to the surface.
- Your ideas remain imaginative and expressive and you match materials to your ideas with purpose and control; well done.

Feedback of this sort can be verbal or possibly written. In both cases the age group you are working with will, to some extent, determine the language you use and how you choose to express your assessment responses. There may be a temptation to reduce the sophistication of your language because the children are 'young'. Being sensitive to their needs is of course appropriate but extending their vocabulary and talking to children with a broad and extensive art and design vocabulary will demonstrate that you take the subject, and their ideas, seriously.

Supportive feedback can be organised and targeted in a number of ways, as identified by the DCSF (2008). References can be made to previous lessons or experiences. Feedback can be focused on processes, knowledge, skills and values, or on review and evaluation. It can be at the beginning of a lesson, or during the lesson, or as part of a lesson review.

PRACTICAL TASK PRACTICAL TASK PRACTICAL TASK PRACTICAL TASK PRACTICAL TASK

Visit the Teacher's TV website and navigate to the art and design videos, choose an example and watch the video. Make observational notes against the categories of feedback identified above. Review your notes and consider how the teacher made good use of specific and non-specific positive feedback.

Examples of feedback

Whole-class feedback
- Last time we worked with clay you will remember we learned the importance of making joints secure and firm by scoring the adjoining surfaces, which many of you did very well.
- We spoke before about reviewing your choices of materials, and trying to match them to your creative intentions. Today I would like you to consider this carefully when you select materials.
- Can we all stop and look this way. Here's a great example of how to combine two different marks with pencils to show texture. Well done, Sean.
- Can anyone identify three things, or characteristics, that these two works of art have in common? And three differences?
- Take a look at our examples of genres of art on the notice board. In which genre would you place this artist's work?

Group feedback
- I've been listening to your group comparing the artists' work, and you've made some good observations. Be a little careful how you talk about colour. *Tone* refers to dark or light, we need another word to describe colour quality, perhaps intensity or hue.
- This group have co-operated particularly well to produce such a convincing image. This isn't easy with lots of different ideas, so well done for making the finished thing look 'united'. By that I mean looking like a team playing well together, not a team of individuals.

Paired feedback
- I like the way you have explained to each other your own ideas and reviewed each other's work fairly but honestly.
- It looks a little bit like you're pulling in different directions. You want to go big and you want more detail, this could be a problem. Any suggestions how you can resolve this difference?

Individual feedback
- I really like the way you have applied this paint, full of energy and joy, just like the music we have listened to.
- Your sketchbook ideas are really lively, and very funny in places. It would be great to see some of this enlarged to a bigger scale, can you imagine that?
- When you mix these paints it is useful to add small amounts of water and paint, to reach the consistency you are looking for. Have I explained the word consistency to you before? Let me try to be a bit clearer by showing you.
- Our objective today was to identify a motif in local architecture and use it as the basis for a repeated print design. Your work reflects this very clearly, well done.

PRACTICAL TASK PRACTICAL TASK **PRACTICAL TASK** PRACTICAL TASK **PRACTICAL TASK**

Add to your observations of the Teacher's TV video an analysis of the focus of supportive feedback against the headings described above. Does the teacher tend to focus on individual or group feedback, or make extensive use of whole class feedback?

Refer to Figure 8.2 on page 132. This teaching encounter was described in *Chapter 6 Considering teachers and teaching: practice* (Figure 6.6, on page 105) and is included here with a focus on assessment and feedback opportunities. Read the encounter again and review the *mysterious shadows* session against the assessment opportunities identified in the chart. For example, consider opportunities to assess use of materials, engagement with processes or ability to review work, and how feedback could support these areas.

Progression and expectations

The *Early Years Foundation Profile Handbook* (QCA, 2008) offers indicators of creative development, accessible via the Standards site: www.standards.dfes.gov.uk

For example at Scale Point 8 it describes creative development where children 'express and communicate ideas, thoughts and feelings using a range of materials and suitable tools'.

An example of this would involve a child, using her knowledge of the properties of materials previously explored to make informed decisions about which materials and tools to use for the purpose or project in mind.

The QCA also offers detailed guidance and examples of progression and expectations within the framework of the National Curriculum, accessible at the Standards site.

They indicate that while levelling and assessment against the National Curriculum attainment targets is not compulsory, its framework is useful for making judgements concerning progress and development.

The QCA suggest that progression in art and design is shown through the different expectations at each key stage. The expectations shown in Figure 8.3 are based on level 2 being the expectation for the majority of children at the end of Key Stage 1 and level 4 being the expectation for the majority of children at the end of Key Stage 2.

The QCA supports in detail an understanding of progression in art and design, in relation to the National Curriculum areas of learning: exploring and developing ideas; investigating and making; evaluating and developing work; knowledge and understanding. Included in Figure 8.4 is an indication of the expected characteristics of Year 6 children in these areas.

Documenting and recording

Although there is no statutory requirement to document individual progress in art and design against National Curriculum attainment target level descriptors, making positive uses of assessment clearly supports learning in art and design.

It is possible that you will encounter a school that keeps profiles of individual work, as indicative examples of National Curriculum expectations. This material may then be used at transition points during primary schooling to support their learning or as evidence to

By the end of **Key Stage 1, most children will be attaining level 2** and will be able to:	By the end of **Key Stage 2, most children will be attaining level 4** and will be able to:
• explore ideas; • investigate and use a variety of materials and processes to communicate their ideas and meanings, and design and make images and artefacts; • comment on differences in others' work, and suggest ways of improving their own.	• explore ideas and collect visual and other information to help them develop their work; • use their knowledge and understanding of materials and processes to communicate ideas and meanings, and make images and artefacts combining and organising visual and tactile qualities to suit their intentions; • compare and comment on ideas, methods and approaches used in their own and others' work, relating these to the context in which the work was made; • adapt and improve their work to realise their own intentions.

Figure 8.3 QCA progression expectations for Key Stage 1 and 2 art and design (www.standards.dfes.gov.uk)

Areas of learning	By the end of Year 6, children:
Exploring and developing ideas	• select and record from experience and imagination, record first-hand observations and explore ideas for different purposes; • make thoughtful observations about starting points and select ideas to use in their work; • select and record visual and other information in a sketchbook and use this to help them develop their ideas.
Investigating and making art, craft and design	• investigate, combine and organise visual and tactile qualities of materials and processes and match these qualities to the purpose of the work; • apply their experience of materials and processes, including drawing, developing control of tools and techniques; • use a variety of methods and approaches to communicate observations, ideas and feelings and design and make images and artefacts.
Evaluating and developing work	• compare and comment on ideas, methods and approaches in their own and others' work and relate these to the context of the work; • adapt and improve their work to realise their own intentions, and describe how they might develop it further.
Knowledge and understanding	• understand visual and tactile elements and how these are combined and organised for different purposes; • understand materials and processes and how these are matched to ideas and intentions; • understand the roles and purposes of artists, craftspeople and designers working in different times and cultures.

Figure 8.4 QCA suggested progression in areas of learning by the end of Year 6 (www.standards.dfes.gov.uk)

Art and Design Development Record	Name: Year group:	
Projects completed:	Indication of level of achievement, including: willingness care thoughtfulness independence awareness	Evidence found: in conversations in sketchbooks in review of work in completed work in individual and group work
Exploring and developing ideas		
Investigating and making		
Evaluating and developing		
Knowledge and understanding		
Working with others		
Working with materials		
Accumulative summary of development:		

adapted from Penny, Ford, Price and Young (2002)

Figure 8.5 Record-keeping format

support reporting to parents or other interested parties. Other schools may keep records of work within their whole-school schemes of work, to show good practice and to keep this evidence to support future teaching and learning, demonstrating what can be achieved with particular age groups.

Photographing work is a particularly useful way of documenting art and design work, and supports teacher- and pupil-focused assessments. You will be able to make use of photographs to support observations of pupil progress, adding to your pupil profile records. Additionally you can use photographs as an integral part of your teaching process, relating pupil experience back to previous encounters. This is a very useful way of sharing learning with children, and helping to remind or refresh ideas.

Photographs of work provide excellent opportunities for children to document and record their own learning experiences. Collecting evidence in sketchbooks, with small printed photographs can be a trigger for reviewing and adapting work. You will be able to support children's art and design vocabulary by providing 'word banks' from which children annotate and review their work, writing and recording thoughts and ideas around, or above, photographs.

Recording achievement and development

From the supporting documentary evidence you will be able to develop an evolving summary of pupil progress, development and achievement. Figure 8.5 is an example adapted from Penny et al. (2002). You will be able to imagine and create your own variation of a record-keeping format, based on the information you wish to record and keep, and in line with school-based experiences of record-keeping profiles.

	Introductory	Threshold	Post-threshold
During the process of working	Join in an art and design lesson, work alongside the class teacher, and support a group of children. Listen to how the teacher gives feedback to individuals and groups, identify useful phrases that you can use.	Working alongside a class teacher, offer some input to an art and design lesson. Offer feedback to individuals and identify areas of development worth sharing with the whole class. Draw the class's attention to these areas.	Working alongside a class teacher or subject leader in art and design, take an active role in teaching the lesson. Make observations of learning across groups and provide feedback which is closely linked to group or individual progress.
Following a period of working	Listen to the class teacher's summary of the lesson and how she provides feedback to children. Discuss with the teacher the progress of children in your group and suggest ways of supporting their development.	Offer feedback to the class at the end of the lesson which motivates them towards future learning. Discuss with the teacher progress across the class and suggest ways to improve and develop the children's work.	Feedback to individuals and groups, paying attention to how the teacher supports needs through peer review and self-evaluation. Encourage children to document their progress, and support with extended vocabulary.
Following extended periods of work	Discuss with class teacher progress of group following a series of lessons. Identify characteristics of work which match QCA level descriptors	Discuss with class teacher progress made by a group of children in relation to level descriptors. Use this information to identify next steps for learning.	Working alongside the class teacher, formulate a series of written feedback statements which reflect your observations of children working and QCA level descriptors. Use this information to support a discussion with parents.

Figure 8.6 Assessment, monitoring and feedback: self-evaluation

Developing your approach to assessment, monitoring and feedback

PRACTICAL TASK PRACTICAL TASK **PRACTICAL TASK** PRACTICAL TASK **PRACTICAL TASK**

Look at and consider Figure 8.6 Assessment, monitoring and feedback. Consider your development needs in terms of assessment, monitoring and feedback, with reference to the *continuum of experience, needs, confidence and support* detailed in the Introduction and developed in *Chapter 5: Considering teachers and teaching: principles*.

The positive approach to assessment, monitoring and feedback considered in this chapter is intended to bridge the sometimes uneasy gap between creative art and design teaching and national frameworks and guidance. The aim, as elsewhere in the book is to help you to support children in the development of their creative art and design responses.

A SUMMARY OF **KEY POINTS**

> **Assessment strategies are varied.**

> **Used positively assessment provides valuable contributions to the process of teaching and learning.**

> **Feedback forms an important part of assessment processes.**

> **Extended vocabulary makes powerful contributions to the feedback process.**

MOVING *ON* > > > **>** **>** **>** MOVING *ON* > > **>** **>** **>** MOVING *ON*

Take this positive approach to assessment into schools and help children to develop their art and design experiences by providing focused feedback.

REFERENCES REFERENCES **REFERENCES** REFERENCES **REFERENCES** REFERENCES

DCSF (2008) Developing oral feedback in art and design available at: http://nationalstrategies. standards.dcsf.gov.uk/node/95507 (accessed 02/05/09).

Eisner, EW (2002) *The arts and the creation of mind*. New Haven, CT: Yale University Press.

Penny, S, Ford, R, Price, L and Young, S (2002) *Achieving QTS: Teaching arts in primary schools*. Exeter: Learning Matters, pp 46–54.

QCA (2008) *Early Years Foundation Stage Profile Handbook*. London: HMSO.

QCA examples of progression and expectations can be accessed at www.standards.dfes.gov.uk (accessed May 2009).

FURTHER READING FURTHER READING **FURTHER READING** FURTHER READING

Barnes, R (2006) *Teaching art to young children 4–9*, 2nd edn. Abingdon: RoutledgeFalmer.

www.curriculum.qca.org.uk

9
Using sketchbooks in the primary school

Chapter objectives

By the end of this chapter you will have:

- **developed your awareness of good sketchbook use;**
- **developed your awareness of the potential for sketchbooks in primary schools;**
- **considered ways of supporting children's sketchbook use;**
- **developed your understanding of assessment, feedback and documentation opportunities in sketchbooks.**

This chapter addresses the following standards for QTS: **Q2, Q7, Q8, Q14, Q15**.

Key themes: investigation; documentation; research; enquiry; development; review; evaluation; children as artists; explore and store.

Introduction

It is acknowledged that good sketchbook use is often indicative of good practice in art and design education. In their subject review, OFSTED (2009) suggest:

> *Where standards were high (in primary art and design education), pupils used sketchbooks frequently and spontaneously, in art lessons and in other subjects. They recorded their observations, developed ideas and experimented with drawing media.*

> (OFSTED, 2009, p7)

This chapter will encourage you to see the potential offered by good sketchbook use in primary art and design. The chapter takes its initiative not only from comments like those of OFSTED (2009), acknowledging frequency and spontaneity, but from the commitment in this book to supporting and valuing children's ideas in art and design. *Chapter 2: Art and design in the primary school: developing the scene, children as artists*, set the tone for this thinking. The chapter suggested that children involve themselves in creative processes similar to those of practising artists. Further chapters have examined ways of supporting children in these creative processes by asking recurring questions about teaching and learning in art and design: 'How can I support inventive and purposeful art and design experiences?'

It is fitting that this final chapter presents a case for the sketchbook as, perhaps, the most appropriate arena for purposeful and inventive art and design experiences; to be explored by children as artists.

Artists and sketchbooks

Sketchbooks offer opportunities to artists to play with ideas, suspend thoughts, imagine new places, document experiences, make mental notes. They are spaces in which to explore the creative and artistic processes described in *Chapter 2: Art and design in the primary school: developing the scene, children as artists*.

In their explorations and representations, creative artists almost always play around with ideas and materials through processes of manipulation, transformation, construction, reshaping or translation. They:

identify, select, construct, combine, assemble, invent, create, explore, develop, investigate, enquire, imagine, represent, reflect, evaluate, present, adapt, modify.

They do so by playing with materials and ideas using a range of productive devices. Amongst other things they:

accumulate	sequence	adapt	combine
select	modify	edit	juxtapose
sort	change	repeat	embellish.

These processes of enquiry echo the creative processes of children and are a powerful way of recognising children as creative artists.

Figure 9.1 Creative and artistic processes

Perella (2004) enthuses about the versatility of the sketchbook when she says 'fortunately, we have discovered an art form completely devoid of rules and absolutely brimming with possibilities' (Perella, 2004, p9). The outcomes of such rule-free endeavour remain as varied and unique as the creators. Some sketchbooks will document an artist's journey of discovery, as they work through ideas, realising those ideas in other more finished forms. A set designer may draw scenes, collect cuttings, or make collages, hinting their way towards a finished and constructed set. A jewellery maker may invest time researching organic forms, taking visual notes with cameras and drawings, adding written annotations about possibilities. They may use tracing techniques to identify and select particular sections, translating them to more polished drawings. The transformation to a piece of silver jewellery may combine ideas from a number of sketchbook sources. A landscape painter may make graphic notes in the field, documenting changing light over several hours or days. Their sketchbooks will form diaries of the changing landscape, its light and the transforming seasons. Back in the studio the landscape painter will compose and craft a more sustained painting, drawing from extensive notes.

There are other artists who choose to maintain their work as sketchbooks. They see the 'book' as an art form itself. They will play with ideas, explore and modify a book's appearance and form, sustaining a considered feel to the overall sketchbook.

Many teachers, who consider themselves artist teachers, keep sketchbooks, not always to form the basis or impetus for more complete work but to sustain a creative appetite, through a discipline of making, invention, enquiry and reflection. The sketchbooks may remain private or be willingly shared with colleagues, peers or pupils.

In the publication *Drawing from life: the journal as art*, New (2005) presents the journals (a broader term which includes diaries, sketchbooks and notebooks) of artists who record systematically their daily and creative lives. These are then presented under the headings observation, exploration, creation and reflection. While these groupings may only be an organisational device in the publication, they are useful as we begin to think about the activities of children in their sketchbooks.

Observation

Cornerstones of many art and design activities, you will be aware that sensing and noticing the world are key features of an art and design education. Artists do this, and then get us to do the same; to remain alert.

In this section we are reminded that some artists use journals and sketchbooks to record in fine detail aspects of marine biology (Jenny Keller), the everyday objects of our lives, hastily drawn in pen and ink (Maira Kellman), carefully noted dreams in images and extensive text (Christopher Leitch), or the almost obsessive mapping of daily routes and journeys over a 23 year period (Masayoshi Nakano).

Exploration

Initiated from travel and journeying, artists use sketchbooks to explore their experiences further. Artists maintain the freshness of a traveller's eyes in their approach to sketchbook pages, where ideas unfold and develop.

In this section artists make use of sketchbooks and drawing to dwell in locations during a year-long cycle journey around the world (Sophie Binder), to make a continuous and open account of a lengthy period in another country, with images, text and montage (Gary Brown), or to adopt a deliberately slow style of writing and drawing with brushes and ink, encouraging unsuspected memories to emerge (Lynda Barry).

Creation

Sketchbooks and journals provide an opportunity for those not familiar with artistic processes to witness them first hand. A place where creative ideas journey towards finished pieces of work.

The sketchbook operates as a tool for creative endeavour. A process which involves artists recording in pencil and watercolour the changing seasonal patterns of suburban gardens (Julie Baugnet), playing with repetition and colour combinations to examine possibilities for quilt making (Denyse Schmidt), or daily sketches in watercolour, extending over 20 years, the 'seed germs' (Holl, in New, 2004, p153) of future architecture.

Reflection

Reflection operates as a critical element of art and design practice, as well as functioning in our daily lives. For some artists, reflective practice is enhanced by rituals: choosing certain materials; acting on a daily basis or setting aside particular times of day; rituals support more carefully-tuned observation and perception.

The sketchbook supports reflective rituals, noticing detail in the often overlooked, photographing each meal eaten over a year from above (Tucker Shaw), hoarding and collaging everyday memorabilia, tickets, text and numbers (Marcy Kentz), or drawing faces and heads from memory and imagination with pen or graphite on small repeated sticky notes (Idelle Weber).

REFLECTIVE TASK

REFLECTIVE TASK

An exhibition featured at the Victoria and Albert Museum in 2008 *'Blood on Paper – the Art of the Book'*, explored the notion of artists' books. It aimed to show the varied way which books have been treated by leading artists of today and the recent past.

The exhibition was diverse showing a range of approaches and production methods. Artists included were, Matisse, Picasso, Braque, Anselm Kiefer, Anish Kapoor, Georg Baselitz, Balthus, Louise Bourgeois, Daniel Buren, Anthony Caro, Eduardo Chillida, Francesco Clemente, Damien Hirst, David Hockney, Sol Lewitt, Richard Long, Robert Motherwell, Robert Rauschenberg and many others.

Visit the website: www.vam.ac.uk/collections/contemporary/bloodonpaper/index.html

Select artists and books which appeal to you and consider their work. Select an image from the artists identified, print it out and note down words associated with the processes identified in Figure 9.1 Creative and artistic processes, and the categories suggested by New (2005), observation, exploration, creation and reflection.

Figure 9.2 Children use sketchbooks to document, observe, explore, create and reflect

Children as artists and sketchbooks

The sketchbook can be an effective way of encouraging children to value their own thinking and learning. The sketchbook can play a key part in preparing ideas, trying out materials and organising thoughts. Sketchbooks provide a space for children to act like creative artists, as shown in Figure 9.2.

When children are given sketchbooks and encouraged to use them in the spirit of artists you may find that it takes time for children to adapt to this sense of playful freedom. However, given time you will notice children getting sketchbooks out during wet play times, taking them home, adding things at the start of the school day or sharing ideas with other children.

You will see children doing all sorts of things. They will have ideas and make explorations, follow investigations and illustrate research. Some of these beginnings may be tentative and will have no other *end*, whereas some can be transformed into more significant or complete art and design work. Some examples are shown in Figure 9.4.

Children as creative artists:

Children do all sorts of things in their homes, on the way to school, in classrooms, on the playground and in sketchbooks which we can consider as being creative. They:

make up songs	turn sticks into weapons	invent words
tell jokes	create secret routes	colour things in
draw pictures	invent games	imagine journeys.

From this short initial list you will get a feel for the creative processes children engage with. They act in ways which are:

playful, imaginative, personal, cultural, emergent, open, flexible, disciplined, skilful, thoughtful, intelligent, engaging, purposeful, practical, inventive, interesting, expressive.

They involve themselves in creative productive processes, where they:

identify, select, construct, combine, assemble, invent, create, explore, develop, investigate, enquire, imagine, represent, reflect, evaluate, present, adapt, modify.

They think and act like creative artists.

Figure 9.3 children as creative artists

Add a page per day	Let things evolve
Bring a drawing in from home	Make up jokes
Collect and sequence events	Make pop-up mouths
Cut out holes	Note things down in decorative text
Draw a series of images	Open up a flap to reveal a message
Design a machine	Question things
Enlarge a section of a photograph	Retell a traditional tale
Fold pages over	Stage a scene from a super-hero adventure
Gather information on a hobby	Test out pens and inks
Have new ideas	Uncover parts of pictures
Imagine and invent creatures	Visualise a favourite poem
Join things together	Work in pairs
Keep a visual diary of a day's events	Wonder what to do next

Figure 9.4 Children and sketchbooks

PRACTICAL TASK PRACTICAL TASK **PRACTICAL TASK** PRACTICAL TASK **PRACTICAL TASK**

Refer to Figure 9.4 Children and sketchbooks. Create your own A–Z list of sketchbook events which you can describe with statements involving action and creative thought.

Using sketchbooks encourages the creative state of mind described by Bentley (2005). In addition, sketchbooks encourage children into the practical and creative processes developed in *Chapter 6: Considering teachers and teaching: practice*, described as the *Productive toolbox*, shown again in Figure 9.5.

Accumulate	Accent
Cut	Arrange
Decorate	Canon
Draw	Categorise
Emboss	Collect
Glue	Combine
Layer	Cover
Loop	Edit
Magnify	Embellish
Mark	Enlarge
Mask	Erase
Order	Expand
Outline	Extract
Paint	Filter
Print	Group
Recur	Juxtapose
Repeat	Map
Sew	Mirror
Stick	Rotate
Stitch	Scale
Trace	Select
Uncover	Sequence
Weave	Sort
Zoom	Wrap

Figure 9.5 Creative and practical processes

Supporting inventive and purposeful sketchbook use

The QCA support the use and development of sketchbooks.

They suggest that children should be encouraged to develop the habit of using their sketchbooks:

- for recording, exploring and storing visual and other information, for example notes and selected materials, which can be readily retrieved and used as reference;
- for working out ideas, plans and designs;
- for reference – as they develop ideas for their work;
- for looking back at and reflecting on their work, reviewing and identifying their progress;
- as an ongoing record of their learning and achievement, which they can use to further develop their ideas, skills and understanding;
- to support talking about their work with others.

Children should develop a range of approaches to using their sketchbooks. These might include using the sketchbook:

- to keep a visual record of their observations made from a range of first-hand sources, such as interesting objects, plant forms, buildings, people. Children should develop and practise the skills of drawing from observation on a regular basis, so that they can increase and sustain their concentration;
- to record a personal response to their experiences and their environment – a way of communicating ideas, feelings and interests;
- as an 'ideas book' where they can explore possibilities and alternatives based on their own ideas and imagination. These may be quirky, odd or impossible and may not necessarily be realised;
- to analyse the methods and techniques used by different artists, craftspeople and designers;
- for visual and annotated notes about line, tone, colour, pattern and so on, for reference for their own creative work;
- for visual and other notes, including personal comments about artists, craftspeople and designers and about particular works that interest them that they study in school and on visits to museums, galleries and exhibitions.

Teachers have an important role to play in supporting and developing the inventive and purposeful use of sketchbooks. They can provide *resources*, make *time* available, offer *feedback*, guide pupil feedback, use a *productive toolbox* to support development, and create a *climate* of purposeful and inventive work.

Resources

The most straightforward thing a teacher can do is to hand out some sketchbooks. They do not need to be over-elaborate or hard-bound with cloth. They come in all shapes and sizes, colours and qualities (although you will be aware that certain papers are more resilient and withstand quantities of sticking and pasting, before falling apart). They take on different names as journals, art books, visual journals, visual notebooks or diaries. They become what the owner wants them to be, or in a classroom they become what teachers and children want them to be. Providing sketchbooks is a positive step towards supporting purposeful and inventive art and design.

Working in sketchbooks with limited resources can liberate creative enquiry, it can also frustrate. As you consider time allocations and possibilities for exploring sketchbook investigations it will be wise to keep in mind the need for other resources. It will be helpful to encourage children to use a particular supply of materials, perhaps stored in a tray or on shelves or in a purpose-made art carry box. This supports a sense of independence; children can monitor and manage materials with increasingly limited teacher interventions. Supporting this supply with good quality materials, and inserting new materials, will sustain interest and offer new directions.

Time

In a busy primary school classroom creating time is very difficult. However, thinking imaginatively about sketchbook use will help you to envisage a range of opportunities. A short burst of 10-minute spells, 3 or 4 times a week, will produce very interesting results. Encouraging children to store wet play time drawings and explorations in sketchbooks for a term will produce themes worth exploring further. Adding a sketchbook slot to the timetable every other week would add to the dynamics of sketchbook use.

Feedback and development

Although many ideas and investigations can be left to sit in sketchbooks, there are times when interventions will support further exploration and enquiry. The *productive toolbox* (after Waters 1994) (see *Chapter 6: Considering teachers and teaching: practice*) is a useful lexicon with which to integrate developmental feedback. You will be able to support further activity and investigation by making suggestions, such as:

- produce a *sequence* of images of your drawings, photocopied and coloured with different combinations;
- *layer* materials to produce qualities of texture and surface;
- *cover* parts of drawings with paper and *mask* areas as you apply coloured materials;
- change the *scale* of your work, *reduce* and *enlarge* on the photocopier;
- *embellish* and *decorate* work using the colour schemes of particular artists;
- *select* a series of images and present them in a *sequence* to show your lunchtime experience;
- *document* the lunchtime experience as a fold-out page in your sketchbook;
- *sort* your favourite toys by size, colour, texture, fabric, colour;
- photograph and *document* each category;
- *cover* your page in graphite, rub out sections with an eraser to *uncover* an image;
- *zoom* in on areas of your drawings.

In some situations teachers support sketchbook work with more direct intervention. Establishing certain expectations, they may ask children to include, or add through their own annotations:

- sketchbook statement;
- the date;
- learning objectives;
- art vocabulary;
- examples of artists' works;
- Well done! stickers;
- self-evaluation comments;
- written feedback comments;
- cross-curricular connections;
- personalised front cover;
- records of visits to galleries, museums and off-site work.

Climate

Although the interventions described above make the process of keeping a sketchbook feel a little more formal, there are some advantages to presenting the sketchbook space with similar authority to other 'books'. As such, children are asked to maintain a sense of discipline when working things out, similar to the discipline identified by many of the artists chronicled by New (2005). In these cases the routine of using a sketchbook instils a sense of purpose, married to the possibility of invention.

This climate, or atmosphere, or ethos, will not happen by chance. It will need your active support and encouragement, praise and reward, demonstration and integrity. This sounds both manageable and reasonable, but achieving this situation will need your input. Possibly the most direct way of supporting a purposeful and *curious classroom* is to use and develop your own sketchbook or journal, where children can see you make mistakes, take up new directions, sustain attention, add detail, reveal new ideas, combine existing ideas, work with unfamiliar materials, or return to favourite resources.

OFSTED (2009) report that:

> *In the most effective (primary art and design) lessons, teachers used their own sketchbooks or collections for discussion and exemplification, or provided confident demonstrations that enabled the pupils to see the artist in the teacher. The teacher's own artistic competence, whether acquired from their own education, through formal training or simply from an appreciation of art, was an important contributor to success.*

(OFSTED, 2009, p13)

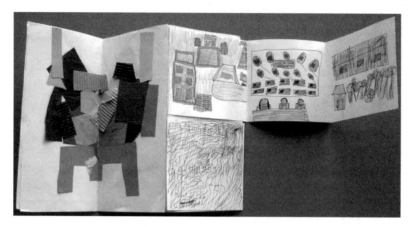

Figure 9.6 Children respond to the challenge of making their own books, in this case 'classroom guidebooks', supported in a climate where ideas are listened to and valued

REFLECTIVE TASK

Seek out an example, by visiting a school or a school website, of sketchbook use in a primary school. Observe and consider the way sketchbooks are used, record your observations against the following areas:

- resources;
- time;
- feedback;
- climate.

To indicate your awareness of what children do in sketchbooks, and how teachers support the use of sketchbooks, did you notice teachers:

- encouraging children to date their work?
- writing objectives on pages of sketchbooks?
- encouraging a range of different work including drawing, painting, textiles, collage, printing, lens-based media and ICT?
- sequencing sketchbook activities to reflect medium-term plans?
- supporting research, experimentation, investigation, reference to visual vocabulary, analysis of artists' works, written self-assessment, evaluation of work with feedback?
- supplying good quality books and materials?
- encouraging children to share their sketchbook ideas?

Refer back to *Chapter 4: Knowledge and understanding: progression of experiences and processes*, identify an art experience and related processes, and related visual qualities. Consider a series of activities which can be developed by children in sketchbooks, encouraging children to explore, investigate, evaluate and develop.

CASE STUDY 9.1

To begin a project about gardens and environments, with his Year 1 class, Mr Martin decided to explore a visual journey. This involved children representing ideas in zigzag books using drawing and collage materials.

Exploring the school grounds and gardens his class stopped at various points, and recorded details of what they saw and experienced in their sketchbooks. They considered colour and shape, noises and other sensations. The children were encouraged to collect found objects in small white envelopes. They made use of coloured pencils, pastels and collage pieces to record findings and observations on luggage tags and a variety of pre-cut A6 papers. Jamie and Isabella were fascinated by a butterfly that fluttered around in the hedge; it seemed to be following them. They set about recording the experience. Jamie picked a red feather from the collage box and stuck it to a luggage tag, while Isabella used brown and red felt-tip pens and recorded a palette of the butterfly's colours.

The activities encouraged children to be inventive and to explore their own ideas. They were able to select their own resources from a collage materials box and a box of drawing materials, carried by Mr Martin and the children along the journey. The children were encouraged to make choices about which materials to use. They made decisions to represent their impressions and thinking about the outside world. They stored and explored their findings in their sketchbooks.

Back in the classroom children were busy selecting pre-cut coloured pieces of sugar paper, measuring about A5 × A2. They watched Mr Martin model the folding of paper into concertina books. He encouraged the children to have a go themselves to create small books for their journeys. Mr Martin helped fold and refold paper where required. A sense of excitement permeated the Year 1 class as they created 'their' books from folded paper.

Page by page children developed their books, separating and determining pages by each stopping point on the journey. Ideas from sketchbooks were translated and transformed, the luggage tags were incorporated, and stencils were used to form text and added to with letter stamps. As the books took shape children worked into the pages embellishments of beads, buttons, sequins and feathers. They contributed further words about things they saw, felt, touched and even imagined!

Printed images of the children experiencing their journey were provided. These added to a final page, incorporating a summary review of the experience from each child.

Assessment, feedback and documentation

The sketchbook provides a useful place to follow development and progression in art and design. When used in appropriate ways they have the possibility to form significant records of experiences, knowledge, skills and creative expression. In particular, sketchbooks are spaces which articulate the sometimes intangible nature of artistic and creative processes. As described in *Chapter 8: Assessment, monitoring and feedback*, sketchbooks provide opportunities to *assess processes and provide feedback*.

It is particularly important to seek out opportunities to comment on and support the learning process involved in art and design. During this process you will see children investigate, explore, try things out, test out ideas, create, invent, imagine, review and evaluate. You will be able to support this process by identifying when, and judging how well, pupils:

- investigate new materials;
- combine materials in inventive and new ways;
- create unusual and imaginative responses;
- explore their ideas;
- challenge their own solutions;
- test out their understanding;
- investigate visual qualities;
- make connections;
- reflect on decisions;
- ask questions.

You can add to your assessments, that pupils do these things well when they are:

- willing;
- consistent;
- independent;
- enthusiastic;
- careful;
- imaginative;
- engaged for sustained periods;
- thoughtful.

It is also possible to follow and determine willingness and ability to engage with evaluation and review. Evidence of this reflective process will be found in the development of practical activity, image making and explorations of visual, tactile and spatial qualities. Children will be seen developing their artistic vocabulary. In addition, children's written commentary can be encouraged and supported in sketchbooks, with direct support from teachers providing vocabulary lists or evaluation writing frames.

Sketchbooks provide opportunities for pupils *to assess, evaluate and review*. The National Curriculum encourages children to review and develop their own work, and to develop their awareness of the work of others. Supporting this sort of review and evaluation is a skilled activity, dependent on teacher interventions which integrate a variety of assessment approaches through prompts, questions and cues. During and after this process you will be able to identify when, and how well, pupils:

- identify visual, tactile and spatial qualities;
- refer to qualities with appropriate language;
- adapt techniques of others;
- edit, adjust or adapt their work;
- adopt techniques of others;
- observe and notice differences or similarities;
- state preferences and dislikes;
- adjust and modify preferences and dislikes;
- ask questions.

You can add to your assessments that pupils do these things well when they are:

- thoughtful;
- considerate;
- sensitive;
- aware;
- alert;
- able to make use of developed language;
- knowledgeable.

It is possible for teachers to add feedback comments to children's sketchbooks. These can be made less intrusive and possibly temporary by making use of sticky notes. The comments can support and champion creative intentions, or be more directed towards skills development or knowledge acquisition. As a summative tool, the sketchbook can be used to provide a powerful example of progress and development across a year group or key stage. However, this chapter supports the creative and artistic use of sketchbooks for purposeful and inventive art and design. We would advise against seeing the sketchbook's purpose as being primarily for assessment opportunities. Doing so would miss the chance for children to engage with 'aesthetic significance' (Hickman, 2005).

PRACTICAL TASK PRACTICAL TASK **PRACTICAL TASK** PRACTICAL TASK **PRACTICAL TASK**

Self-evaluation

Look at and consider Figure 9.7 Using sketchbooks and self-evaluation. Consider your development needs in terms of using sketchbooks in primary schools, with reference to the *continuum of experience, needs, confidence and support* detailed in the Introduction and developed in *Chapter 5: Considering teachers and teaching: principles*.

A SUMMARY OF **KEY POINTS**

> **Sketchbooks can support inventive and purposeful art and design.**

> **Children can explore their own ideas in sketchbooks with creative and varied outcomes.**

> **Sketchbooks are a place to store and explore these ideas, and a place where teachers can provide feedback and comment to develop ideas further.**

> **Sketchbooks can be used to support assessment and feedback opportunities in art and design.**

	Introductory	Threshold	Post-threshold
Personal engagement with sketchbooks	Kept a sketchbook in school, as directed to by art and design teacher.	Kept a personal sketchbook to support further learning. Some awareness of artists' use of sketchbooks. Awareness of resources to develop knowledge and understanding of sketchbooks.	Continued use of sketchbooks to record creative and visual journey for personal and professional use. Real understanding of the value of sketchbooks to experiment and investigate and support the development of ideas. Development of own sketchbook and an appreciation of the work of others' sketchbooks in schools and the world of art and design.
Experience of sketchbooks in schools	Aware of sketchbooks being present in classes. Some use directed by teacher, but without understanding and appreciation of application to sequence of work.	Identified a range of sketchbooks across year groups and key stages. Analysed the contents and methodology. Used sketchbooks with children during an art and design lesson to investigate and experiment for a project.	Looked at a sample of sketchbooks in schools. Planned to use good practice seen in own approach, together with developing own sketchbook to model in the classroom. Used books with children to creatively inspire thinking and enhance experiences and skills. Time given for development of work in sketchbooks.
Development opportunities to use sketchbooks with children	With guidance plan a lesson to use sketchbooks. Plan for opportunities for support, development and and reflection.	Use sketchbooks involving an art and design activity to fit into the sequence of previous and future lessons. Incorporate expectations and challenges for experimentation and development of ideas. Support work with feedback.	Develop the imaginative use of sketchbooks with a range of activities supported with personal examples and discussion. Incorporate experimental and investigative activities, reflecting a sequence of lessons. Develop support for self-evaluation.

Figure 9.7 Using sketchbooks: self evaluation

MOVING *ON* > > > > > > MOVING *ON* > > > > > > MOVING *ON*

Make or purchase a sketchbook. Take on board the ideas in the chapter and take them, along with your sketchbook, into your next school placement.

REFERENCES REFERENCES **REFERENCES** REFERENCES **REFERENCES** REFERENCES

Bentley, T (2005) *So Giotto drew on rock: Children's right to art and everyday democracy*. Available at: www.demos.co.uk/publications/sogiottodrewonrocks (accessed 02/05/09).

Hickman, R (2005) *Why we make art and why it is taught*. Bristol: Intellect Books.

Victoria and Albert Museum (2008) *Blood on paper – the art of the book*. Available at: www.vam.ac.uk/collections/contemporary/bloodonpaper/index.html (accessed 02/05/09).

New, J (2005) *Drawing from life: The journal as art*. New York: Princeton Architectural Press.

Ofsted (2009) *Drawing together: Art craft and design in schools 2005–08*. London: Ofsted.

Perella, L (2004) *Artists' journals and sketchbooks: exploring and creating pages*. Gloucester, MA: Quarry Books.

QCA offer suggestions for the use of sketchbooks in the framework of the National Curriculum, accessible at the Standards site www.standards.dfes.gov.uk

FURTHER READING FURTHER READING **FURTHER READING** FURTHER READING

Kelly, K (ed) (2007) *1000 journals project*. San Francisco, CA: Chronicle Books.

Robinson, G (1995) *Sketchbooks explore and store*. London: Hodder & Stoughton.

Wasserman, K and Drucker, J (Eds) (2006) *The book as art: Artists' books from the National Museum of Women in the Arts*. New York: Princeton University Press.

www.drumcroon.org.uk/Sketchbooks/sketch.html

From the Drumcroon website some valuable examples of artist's and educators' sketchbooks.

http://www.accessart.org.uk/sketchbook/

An inspirational site for sketchbook use in schools, full of ideas, images, video clips, children's work.

Conclusion

To support you in teaching of primary art and design, we have covered a range of ideas, developed them with examples from theory and from practice, and illustrated them with scenarios from school-based encounters. Working through this material has asked you to consider the recurring theme of helping children with purposeful and imaginative art and design experiences and response.

If you take on board the responsibility of helping children, with enthusiasm and interest, goodwill and integrity, the rewards will be plentiful. You will see children excited by the prospect of engaging with interesting and varied materials, challenged by new combinations of resources, intrigued and baffled by the work of varied and exciting artists, craftspeople and designers. You will see them work out in sketchbooks ideas which are stimulating and humorous. You will see children make delicate and intricate patterns with pens and coloured pencils. You will see them feeling proud of large-scale group work.

These rewards are, of course, a feature and privilege of teaching, but the real rewards rest with children; it is for their benefit that we teach art and design in educational settings. Doing so provides opportunities for children to seek out meaningful and purposeful learning; to find opportunities of 'aesthetic significance', where 'through making, experimenting with materials and critically engaging with a range of visual forms, people celebrate their humanity' (Hickman, 2005, p174).

Primary art and design is worth teaching well.

REFERENCES REFERENCES **REFERENCES** REFERENCES **REFERENCES** REFERENCES
Hickman, R (2005) *Why we make art and why it is taught*. Bristol: Intellect Books.

Added to a page number 'f' denotes a figure